This Life of Grace

Stranger on the Shore

This highly unusual book tells the story of an ordinary Cornish family affected over generations by an appalling genetic disease, and by the nightmare of not knowing who it will strike next. Yet there is a kind of triumph amid the suffering. The sensitive writing on a subject that could hardly be more serious makes for an unforgettable read.

PEOPLE'S BOOK PRIZE REVIEW

JOHN SYMONS spent the first two years of his life in India, and the next sixteen in Devon and Cornwall.

Fluent in Russian and described by a former British Ambassador to Russia as an 'enthusiastic Russophile', he is working on a book about the effects of Bolshevism on Russia and Communism on Great Britain. He also writes short stories and poems.

This Life
of Grace

JOHN SYMONS

SHEPHEARD-WALWYN (PUBLISHERS) LTD

First published in 2011 by
Shepheard-Walwyn (Publishers) Ltd
107 Parkway House, Sheen Lane,
London SW14 8LS
www.shepheard-walwyn.co.uk

British Library Cataloguing in Publication Data
A catalogue record of this book
is available from the British Library

ISBN: 978-0-85683-283-3

Typeset by Alacrity, Chesterfield, Sandford, Somerset
Printed and bound in the United Kingdom
by the Blisset Group of London

For Judy
who suggested this book
many years ago

We lived alongside her,
but all of us failed to grasp that she was
that one truly just person
without whom, as the saying goes,
no village is safe,
nor any town,
nor our whole world.

A.I. SOLZHENITSYN
Matryona's House
(Author's translation,
used by permission of
Mrs Natalia Solzhenitsyn)

Still are thy pleasant voices, thy nightingales,
  awake;
For Death, he taketh all away, but them he
  cannot take.

W.J. CORY
Heraclitus

Contents

Prologue   ix

PART ONE

1 'When you and I were seventeen'   3

Confirmation, November 1924   19

2 'Dear Octopus'   20

3 'Tea at Gunters'   27

4 'The test of the heart is trouble'   36

5 'The best thing that ever happened to me'   49

PART TWO

6 '…down to Oxford's towers'   53

7 A New Life   55

8 Windwhistle   67

9 Neighbours and Friends   70

10 A Pattern of Life   85

11 Time Passes   92

12 'Gone are the days…'   101

PART THREE

13 A Last Gift   117

    Ward 12, Mount Gould Hospital   121

14 'What can't be cured...'   122

    Winged Chariot   132

15 '...on my way, rejoicing'   133

16 'A Ring of Faithfulness'   138

    Skin Deep   146

17 'Such sweet sorrow'   147

Epilogue   *...the means of grace and the hope of glory...*   150

Prologue

ON AN IRON-FRAMED BED, in a side room off Ward 12, Grace lies on a Pegasus air mattress. The electric motor of an air-compressor hums very quietly and, every so often, it gently inflates or deflates one or another of the lungs of the mattress. The 'Friends of Ward 12' have raised the money for the hospital to buy more of these mattresses. Ward 12 is a special place. It has many grateful friends. The flow of air changes the contours of the bed and reduces the risk of bedsores. Grace was already suffering from one when she was moved to the specialist unit here from a ward in a general hospital.

Outside, about sixty feet from the window of her little room, stands an immense horse chestnut tree, covered in fresh green leaves. The first white and saffron flowers are opening. Grace watched the tree's leaves turn brown and fall, along with the conkers, last autumn. She saw the tree's branches bare against the blue winter sky. You can look at a tree for a long time.

Grace has lain on this bed for six months. Every two hours or so, she is turned from one side to the other by members of a group of skilled and dedicated nurses and assistants. She is paralysed on her left side, the effect of the stroke that she suffered in September. She cannot feed or clean herself.

Grace's speech is a little slow, soft but clear. Sometimes her mind is muddled, but often it is completely lucid. Sometimes she sleeps deeply, sometimes fitfully. After a deep sleep this morning, her mind is alert.

'I've been over nearly all of it now,' she tells me. *'I'm happy.'*

Grace is my Mother.

This is the story of her long life, what she was turning over in her mind. It is what made her happy. It is what she told me during her thirty-two months in Ward 12, between her stroke and her death. She was amused, and perhaps pleased, that I noted down what she was saying in a shorthand book. We called it her 'log'. Many of the words of this story are hers.

PART ONE

1

'When you and I were seventeen'

IT WAS THERE from the beginning.

No one could tell how the story would end and no one would have wanted it to end as it did, but what was there from the beginning made the end possible and gave it its meaning.

Mum was born in October 1909 into a large, united family. Descended from generations of farm labourers and game-keepers, her parents and many of her uncles and aunts had gone 'into service' as butlers and valets, cooks and maids during the sixty-three years of Queen Victoria's reign.

Not long after King George V came to the throne in 1910, Mum's family moved from Cornwall to Plymouth in south Devon. For a while, as an alternative to domestic service, her parents ran a sweet-shop, but they could not make it pay. Perhaps it was as a toddler, in the sweetshop, that Mum gained her life-long taste for liquorice and chocolate.

Two years later the family moved from the city to the village of Plympton St Mary, where Mum's father once more earned his living as a butler.

3

'*The first thing I remember was being in the back lane of our row of houses, a bit lonely as all the other children had gone in a horse-and-wagon on the chapel outing to the seaside at Wembury,*' Mum told me.

'*My next memory was of one breakfast-time, jumping up when Mother was making my cocoa, knocking a kettle of water over my shoulders. All the family rushed around frantically trying to help poor Mother. The district nurse came and did my wound. I lay in a cot in the kitchen, being spoiled once more. Mother slept on a mattress on the floor by my cot for a few nights.*'

Mum always looked at her parents through rose-tinted spectacles. '*I can't help doing it,*' she told me. But her memories contain nuggets that run counter to the way she wished to see things. The stories that she passed on reveal that she had a formidable power of recall and was an honest witness. Her memories have always proved to be accurate when it has been possible to check them.

Mum started school on the thirty-first of August 1914, one day short of four weeks after the First World War broke out, and two months before her fifth birthday.

'*Starting school was a shock to me, being the youngest of eight and a bit spoiled by the others. My sister Hilda was ten years older than me and had already left school. She took me to the baby school, called Bridge School in those days, at the foot of Station Hill. She told me to run home, and told Mother that she hadn't been able to catch me. The next day Mother took me, and, very tearfully clutching a packet of chocolate drops, I was left with Mrs Bettes and Miss Blight ...*

'*Our house in Moorland View was lovely. A few weeks later at Christmas, it was filled with holly and ivy, and we just had stockings filled with simple presents, and oranges, apples, and nuts. We had a lovely Christmas dinner and Christmas pudding (set alight with brandy), with ten of us around the table. Two doors away lived my friend, Edie Law, and we always had a good Christmas, with our dolls and toys ...*

'We had baths on Saturdays in a tin bath in front of the kitchen fire; there was no bathroom there. After the bath we had sweets.'

Sixty years later, out of the blue, Edie Law visited Mum.

'Yesterday was a strange day. I answered the doorbell. A lady and a gentleman stood there, and the lady said, "Can you tell us where to find 14 Moorland View where I used to live?" I gave a shout, "Edie Law!" and she said, "Grace Jarrold!" We had not met for sixty years. She was my playmate. They came in and had cups of tea and coconut buns (I didn't have anything else). They stayed two and a half hours and we talked the hind leg off a donkey, about all the games that we played and of the people we knew. They live in Bristol. Edie's husband was tickled pink at our meeting. It was very funny after all those years.'

Another of Mum's friends in Moorland View was Edie Paul. At school Edie was a lively pupil. Like her brother Bill, Edie had the bluest eyes that Mum ever saw. Once, the teacher tried to get her to concentrate, saying 'Edith Paul, put on your thinking-cap.' Edie replied, 'I can't, Miss; I've only got my 'shanter'.

During Mum's first years at school her two eldest brothers were in the Army, serving in France.

'I remember Mother crying when Harry and Jack went to war. When they came back from the front on leave their uniforms were filthy from the mud of the trenches and full of fleas. Mother used matches to get the fleas to jump out of the serge; the cloth was so thick and that was the only way to get rid of them.'

After the United States entered the Great War two Americans were billeted with her family for several months in late 1917 and 1918. Mum was frightened of them because they used to play boisterously with her, throwing her up into the air and catching her. *'Yanks'*, as she often called them, rather fondly, always amused her by their *'exuberance'*, a favourite word of hers.

Food was short. According to the log-book kept by the headmaster of the senior school, called Geasons, his staff and pupils

used to grow an annual crop of potatoes during the War and
for a good few years after it, partly for food and partly to teach
the children how to work a vegetable garden. The area under
cultivation at the school in 1917 was seven and three quarter
roods, a plot that amounts to almost two acres. In the spring
of that year Geasons' staff and pupils planted a hundredweight
of seed potatoes.

A series of small events and treats marked the passing of
each term. In the late spring and summer months the parish
church of St Mary, and the Wesleyan and Congregationalist
chapels in Ridgeway, as the high street was called, used to
organise teas and outings for the children of the village. On
those days the schools would be closed.

Not far from the school stood Hillside House where General
and Mrs Birdwood lived for many years. They offered Geasons
great support. In early summer each year they gave a tea party
for the children in their large garden, with its forest of shrubs
and rhododendrons. The wisteria would be in full bloom,
covering the south front of the house.

Mr Baple, the energetic new headmaster, recorded in his
log-book on the morning of Empire Day, the 24th of May 1917,
that 'Suitable lessons were given and General Birdwood gave
a brief address to the children on "The Empire and the Flag".'
In the words of the writer of a recent textbook,* 'The British
Empire... stretches over the whole globe... The sun never sets
or rises over the British dominions... It would be perfectly
possible to put round the earth a girdle of telegraphic wire, the
ends of which should rest only upon land that belongs to
the British Empire.' Another recent popular history for
children told 'Our Empire Story'.[†]

The pride felt in our country's history and achievements
was combined with humour and a sense of proportion. On the
same day that General Birdwood gave the pupils his talk on

---

* J.M.D. Meiklejohn, *A New History of England and Great Britain*, 1902.
† By Miss H.E. Marshall.

the Empire, Mr Baple noted in his log that there was 'a small attendance of children in the afternoon, a circus being in Plympton'.

The following year on St George's Day, the twenty-third of April, there were lessons 'suitable to the day'. A collection in the school raised £1 0s 3d, for the RSPCA's fund for horses wounded in the War.

Plympton St Mary was a loyal, quiet village. It was home to three or four thousand people, including those living in the neighbouring smaller villages of Plympton St Maurice and Colebrook and in the outlying hamlets. There was a spirit of patriotism in the village and school, and of long-suffering, stoical humanity and realism, with modest pleasures and no luxuries.

The village was typical of thousands across the country. That the people of our country were once so gentle and patient, so hardy and decent, so reasonable and free, facing together so many hardships, can hardly be believed by anyone born after 1950, but so it was.

Even those on the fringes of society in Mum's childhood seemed to share in this powerful ideal as much as anyone else.

Tramps were sometimes seen passing through Plympton on the main road between Exeter and Plymouth. Without irony, they were known as 'gentlemen of the road'. One of them regularly called on Mum's family. Her mother would give him tea, some food to take on his way and a pair of boots saved up for his visit. Sitting at the kitchen table, he used to tell Mum and her mother of his adventures on his long walk between John o'Groats and Land's End. Even when she was elderly, perhaps partly as a result of this friendship, which lasted for many years, Mum used to carry some loose change with her in her mackintosh pocket in case she met a tramp *in need of a cup of tea*.

Old-fashioned gipsy caravans sometimes visited the village. Once in a while they made an encampment in the field beside the Tory Brook, between St Mary's church and the livestock

market. Fascinated by the sight, the village children watched
them cooking on their camp-fires and putting their children
to bed under the stars. When one of the gipsies died, he was
sent on his way by a large congregation at a funeral service in
St Mary's.

In the autumn of 1918 as the Great War was coming to its
end, an influenza epidemic (known as 'Spanish 'flu') began to
rage in the country. In Plympton only sixty per cent of the
children were able to attend school on some days. At the end
of October and in early November Mr Baple closed the school
completely for a fortnight. One boy, Robert Parsons, died.
The pupils brought in their pennies for a wreath; £1 6s 11d was
collected. Later they made a contribution to the costs of his
funeral.

The following summer, in mid-July, the school held a special
celebration to mark the return of peace. Mum won a prize in
the sports which took place in Geasons field. The next day,
according to Mr Baple's notes, 'the cake remaining from the
festivities was distributed among the children'. Mum's family
had a photograph taken of them all gathered together in their
back-garden.

'At the King's express desire', the midsummer holiday
was extended from four to five weeks that year. The country,
including the children, could begin to breathe more easily for
a while.

That summer Mum's brother, Walter, three years her senior,
won a scholarship to Corporation Grammar School at North
Road in Plymouth.* He was a clever boy, and the first in the

---

* Plympton Grammar School had been closed in the early nineteenth century.
  Sir Joshua Reynolds, the portrait painter and first President of the Royal
  Academy, and Plympton's most distinguished son, had been educated there.
  It was re-opened in Plympton St Maurice in 1921, too late for Wally, so his
  family had the additional expense of his train fares to Plymouth every day.
  The school was moved to a new building in Plympton St Mary, still in use
  but much extended, in September 1937. It is now known as Hele's School,
  in commemoration of one of the original benefactors.

family to go to a grammar school. The family had just enough money to pay for the uniform and books that he needed. Mum's father was working as the butler at Newnham House, a mile outside the village. He earned 23 shillings a week (£1 15p). Apart from Wally, Mum's brothers and sisters were by now in work.

In September Wally took up his scholarship. Mum moved up the hill from Bridge School to Geasons. There were about three hundred children at the school, 135 of them boys and 154 girls.

Mum's family bought her new clothes for the move to the senior school: a warm winter coat, a hat and gloves, and leather lace-up boots. Winters were usually severe and long, and Mum always suffered from chilblains.

'I remember going up to the Big School. I really loved it when I got used to it, especially when I got older, although I went up the hill from the baby school shaking in my shoes on the first day.'

At the end of October the pupils subscribed £1 2s 10d for a portrait of Nurse Edith Cavell. The matron of a hospital in Brussels at the start of the War, Nurse Cavell had become a popular heroine. She had risked her life by helping two hundred British and Allied soldiers to escape to The Netherlands after the German army occupied Belgium in 1914. She was executed by the Germans in 1915. Her picture was placed in the school's main assembly room.

On the eleventh of November 1919, the first national commemoration of the anniversary of the Armistice, Mr Baple wrote in his diary: 'An Assembly was held in the Schoolroom, in accordance with the King's desire. Silence at 11am for a few minutes; then an address on the subject of the day – the Armistice, its results, the League of Nations, etc. School closed in the afternoon'.

At the end of the winter, in early 1920, Bridge and Geasons Schools were inspected by His Majesty's Inspectorate of Education. The Inspector, Mr A.M. Morley, reported:

'The discipline, which during the war years at times showed unsteadiness, is now much improved and the staff more settled than it was. The majority of the children are bright and intelligent, though there are a few very dull ones who seem to need special attention. The subjects of instruction as seen at the time of the visit appear on the whole to be up to the average, and the methods of teaching are generally suitable, although this is more characteristic of the upper than the lower part of the school.

'It is clear that the organisation might be improved in certain details which were discussed with the Head Master at the time of the inspection, and the timetable which has been in use a long time needs revision. The scheme of work, which was drawn up some years ago, is too vague and general in character to be of much help to the assistant teachers, and the terminal examinations might well cover a wider range of subjects.

'In a school of this size, the children in Standard VII (thirteen year olds) should attempt more advanced work by means of private study instead of, as at present, working with Standard VI and occasionally Standard V.'

Althia Birdwood countersigned the report of the inspection on behalf of the governors.

By now Mum had just passed her tenth birthday. She had a little less than four years' schooling ahead of her. There were about forty-five children in her class. Mum loved school and worked hard at her lessons.

Perhaps as a result of the inspector's report the school began to arrange for more of its pupils to sit the scholarship examination for the grammar school.

Mum did well in her studies. *'When I was thirteen, I was made head girl, and every morning at eleven o'clock I used to fetch Mr Baple his coffee on a tray from the cottage in Station Road where he and Mrs Baple lived.'*

Mr Baple encouraged Mum's parents to put her in for a scholarship to the grammar school. Nothing came of his idea. There was not enough money for the family to buy Mum the uniform and anything else that she would have needed for the extra two years at the grammar school to take her school certificate.

'I didn't have the nerve to go in for the scholarship although Mr Baple told me that I could easily pass. I wasn't brave enough – too babyish, I expect. My family were too nice to me; I can't get away from that – they spoilt me.'

Mum always looked back to her days at school with Mr Baple with affection. In 1976, when she was reading *Devon Life,* she told me, *'I saw a letter by my old schoolmaster, Mr W.H. Baple. He asked pupils of 1919 to 1923 to write to him. I have done so and eagerly await a reply. He says that he has been in India. I told him all the news and hope that he will enjoy reading about my time in India with Dad. You cannot believe the thrill I got from seeing his name.'*

Mum would have done well at the grammar school. She never gave the slightest hint of resenting her loss. Even with most of her brothers and sisters already at work, she could see that her family's funds were short.

So it was that Wally was the first and last of that generation to enjoy a grammar school education. Mum was proud of his success. She cried when, near the end of her life, she told me that on one occasion some pupils in Plymouth had jeered at him because of the patches and darns in his school uniform, lovingly and carefully mended by their mother.

Mum made the most of the schooling that she received. Mrs Bettes had given her a few piano lessons when she was at Bridge School, and now she started to take regular lessons with Mr Leonard Ash at Geasons.

'Mr Ash made me blush when he called me out to the front to play a piece to the class.'

A little later, Mum began to take piano lessons with Miss Chubb in the dark drawing-room of her house, hidden behind a dense laurel hedge, in the terrace where Mr and Mrs Baple lived. Miss Chubb used to smack her hand with a ruler if she made a mistake. It did not often happen. She encouraged Mum

to go on to 'take theory', saying that she would become an
excellent musician if she did so. Although there was no money
for the extra lessons for that, Mum always played well, with
feeling and accuracy. She won a music prize.

There was a good teacher of English at Geasons, Mrs
Markham, and she encouraged her pupils to read some of the
great works of English literature. Mum relished learning
poetry. For all her shyness, she enjoyed reciting or performing
it: Wordsworth's *Idle Shepherd Boys*, Tennyson's *The Brook* and
The Revenge, and passages from Shakespeare's *The Merchant of
Venice*, including Portia's speech in praise of mercy (her lifelong
favourite). All the books that Mum read at school and in later
years lived on in her heart and mind, stored there by her
powerful memory, imprinting their lessons on her soul. Each
term there were examinations in arithmetic, in reading and
in the writing of compositions or essays.

Every week Mum used to go with Sam, her family's spaniel,
to take the rent to Mrs Damerell, the farmer's wife who owned
the house. Mrs Damerell told Mum how much she admired
Mrs Jarrold for keeping the house so clean and looking so neat
and tidy, with the ten of them living there. But now Mum's
family had to move. In the economic confusion that followed
the Great War Mrs Damerell had to sell the house to raise
money to enable her husband, who was much older than
herself, to save the farm.

So in 1922, twelve months before Mum left school, the
Jarrolds went to live on a small council estate of red-brick
houses, newly built for soldiers returning from the Great War
– 'homes fit for heroes' as they were known – a little to the
northwest, on the far side of the valley and the railway line.
Their house, Number 7 Stone Barton, would stay in the family
for more than sixty years.

Despite the new houses, Plympton remained peaceful and
little changed. The population rose to about five thousand by

the mid-1920s. *'They were days when you could walk in the fields and roll in the daisies and buttercups without being molested,'* she told me in 1990, when the papers reported that a murder had been committed in Plympton.

'We had simple treats. I remember Mother and her sister, Aunt Emily, taking us in a donkey cart to Wembury to see the sea. Sometimes Jakey the donkey would not move, and Mother stood in front encouraging him with carrots.'

When I went to Bulgaria in 1993 and visited the depths of the countryside on local trains, I wrote to Mum to tell her about life there. She replied that it sounded like Plympton in her childhood, *'with donkeys and carts and hayricks and people living very simply'*.

At home, Mum was still treated as the baby of the family. *'I was still playing with dolls when I was thirteen years old,'* she told me. She was amused and a little ashamed that she had been so slow to grow up.

Mum left school with a good report, as well as with her prizes. *'I left school a few months before I was fourteen. I had won a prize for my work. Mrs Birdwood presented me with it, a book called* The Flower of the Family. *She said to me,* "I hope that you will be the flower of your family."'

Mr Baple wrote in Mum's report, 'I cannot praise her too highly as a gifted and dutiful pupil.'

Some of the girls at school were jealous of Mum's success and teased her. They said that Mr Baple was 'not praising her'. Mum knew that Mr Baple had given her a good report from what he had said to her, but she was upset when she told her parents what the girls had said. Her mother and father assured her that Mr Baple had, indeed, given her a wonderful report.

In the autumn of 1923 Mum started work. There was little choice of jobs. Years later she told me, *'If I had my time again, knowing what I know now, I would have gone on with botany.'* She loved to search for flowers and plants in the fields, woods and hedges and identify rare finds in the well-thumbed books handed on by her parents.

At another time she pondered a different possibility. It was when she was travelling to Moorhaven Hospital three times a week to visit Dad. She got to know the Matron of one of the Plymouth hospitals who said that she would be pleased to offer Mum a job. *'The nurses are so kind and thoughtful to all the patients, and, if I had my time again, I would try to be a nurse. They are so wonderful.'*

Mum's two sisters were by now well into their twenties. Like their parents before them they had gone 'into service'. There were twenty or so substantial country houses in the rich farming country around Plympton offering such work, and Edie and Hilda 'lived in' as maids. Things were beginning to change even then in the early 1920s. Because of the slump in farming, the landed families were cutting back on servants. Perhaps Mum's mother felt that her youngest was too young for her years and too home-loving to move out and live with other servants in a country house and work for a strange family.

Whatever the reason, Mum took a different route. In August 1923 she began to work at Northcott's, a small drapery shop in Ridgeway. She received 3s 9d (19p) a week. She gave her mother three shillings; the nine pence that she kept, she spent on a bun or a slice of Russian cake and a glass of milk at Mr Heathman's dairy, or liquorice at Mrs Gent's sweetshop.

Mum enjoyed her work at Northcott's. She became fond of the elderly spinster who ran the shop. She observed her fussy manners and took in her droll words about her customers. She stored it all away.

Mum always loved Ridgeway, and that love went back to her childhood. *'I was happy with life as it was. If we wanted a treat, we just went to Ridgeway. You wouldn't believe that would you? And it was so nice when the Christmas tree was set up there and covered with lights.'*

She was disappointed when the earliest known painting of Plympton, by William Tomkins in the mid-eighteenth century, was sold to an American and exported in 1990.

The confirmation service at St Mary's church was a big event each year, especially for the school-leavers.

In November 1924, when she was fifteen, Mum was one of the thirty-nine parishioners confirmed at St Mary's. The Bishop who conducted the service preached on a text from the Book of Revelation, *'Be faithful unto death,'* words inscribed on the flyleaf of the small prayer book presented to each of the candidates.

Until about 1960 around half of the local school-leavers were confirmed each year in Plympton, between forty and sixty of them. Several adults would also be confirmed. In those fifteen years after the Second World War the ways and manner of life in the village were more like those of the 1920s and 1930s than what followed.

After working at Northcott's for a few months Mum moved to a more promising job at Yeo's department store in Plymouth. Her mother had taken her to Plymouth to buy an apprenticeship at one of the stores in the city. The first shop that they visited was Dingles, *'But I wasn't smart enough for Dingles,'* Mum said, *'so we settled on Yeo's.'*

In the old city of Plymouth, destroyed by German bombs twenty years later, Yeo's ranked below Pophams and Dingles, but on a level with Spooner's and above Coster's among the big department stores, all of which stood in, or near, Bedford Street.

The choice of Yeo's turned out well for Mum and she made the most of her opportunity. She made some friendships which lasted a lifetime. Lily Coombes, two years older than Mum, was already working there. The apprenticeship gave her training in each department in turn. She loved the shop and the daily routine. Each morning she travelled from Plympton station on the 8.40 train to North Road station. *'There were a lot of smart girls on the train. One worked at Pophams.'* Normally she took the short walk from there to Yeo's, although from time to time she caught a tram.

At midday, when the weather was fine, she used to buy a sandwich or pasty at the Three Towns Dairy or the Windsor Dairy in George Street. With her friends, she would walk up to The Hoe and they would eat their lunch looking out over the waters of Plymouth Sound.

Mum still felt very young for her years: *'I was a thin little girl standing behind the counter – very skinny. Some days I wore a long-sleeved white jumper that was almost too tight at the neck to pull over my head; it shrank each time it was washed. I felt like two yards of pump-water.*

'At first I used to earn ten shillings (50p) a week. I used to give the brown envelope to Mother: she had a lovely way of receiving and giving. Then, at the end of the apprenticeship, my wages went up to £1 a week. To celebrate this increase Mother bought me a grey flannel suit with a waistcoat, and a Scottish 'shanter with a tassel, at a shop in Old Town Street. I felt lovely in that outfit.'

Mum became popular at Yeo's. The owner, Major Frank Yeo, 6' 4" tall and distinguished in bearing, used to tease her. 'You have grown a lot since I last saw you', he said when he told her of her increase to £1 a week. Mum's height of 5' 10" made her noticeable in those days when most young women were so much shorter than they are now. The manager, John Beckley, also used to pull her leg. 'You are fit only for the carpet department', he said and she pretended to be furious.

On Wednesdays, when the shops closed for a half-day, Mum sometimes went to the pictures with a friend. Saturday was a full working day.

The other girls working at Yeo's were interested in Mum's big family. 'How many brothers have you got, Jarrold?' they asked her. (The girls used each others' surnames at work.) When she replied, *'Five,'* they asked, 'Can we come out to Plympton and see you next Wednesday afternoon?'

Once a week, after work, her mother used to go into Plymouth on the 5.09 train. Mum would treat her to tea at Goodbody Matthews' café in George Street, near St Andrew's Cross. Mum would feel so proud of her when one of the girls called out, 'Your mother has arrived, Jarrold.'

They would drink a pot of tea or small cups of strong coffee with cream, and eat tiny, delicate sandwiches and delicious cakes which they used to share, half each, so that each of them tasted everything. A string trio, made up of tall, thin ladies with reading-glasses and long noses would play light classical and salon music: Kreisler's *Caprice Viennoise*, Paderewski's *Minuet in G* and *Chanson du Voyageur*, Elgar's *Chanson de Matin*. There was a certain homeliness, but with a hint of romance, even elegance, in the busy, thriving city.

The two of them would then go to the pictures at the Gaumont Cinema or Andrews Picture House in Union Street. They often saw dramatisations of classic novels, *Wuthering Heights, The Hunchback of Notre Dame,* and *Anna Karenina. The Barretts of Wimpole Street* was a favourite. They used to catch the 9.20 train back to Plympton station.

Mum's father worried about her. One day, when she was seventeen and was dressed up *'to go out flirting, Dad took me aside. I was wearing a black coat with an astrakhan collar and a French cloche hat. Dad told me that I looked like a "Piccadilly Pat". Dad was stern in my flirting days.'*

'I was a perfect nuisance when I was seventeen,' Mum told me. *'I used to keep Mum and Dad up late, till eleven o'clock, when I was out flirting. I fell for the curate at St Mary's, but I didn't dare to speak to him. I was seventeen and he was forty...*

'Mr Brooks used to cut my hair with a fringe, or a shingle, or an Eton crop, at his shop in Ridgeway...

'My brothers paid for me to have my first filling at the dentist's – Mr Arthur James – in Plymouth. They wanted me to have good teeth.'

One day nearly seventy years later, Joan Vincent, one of Mum's oldest friends from Stone Barton, visited her in Ward 12. They talked about the old days. Together they sang one of the songs from a pantomime that they had seen at the Palace Theatre so long ago:

> *'When you and I were seventeen,*
> *And love and life were new,*
> *The world was just a field of green,*
> *With smiling skies of blue,*
> *That lovely spring when you were King*
> *And I was then your Queen;*
> *Can you recall when love was all,*
> *And we were seventeen?'**

Mum enjoyed her time at Yeo's. She loved dealing with customers and selling them hats and flowers, shirts and hosiery. She was unhappy for a while in the despatch department. One of the staff there was dishonest and tried to lead her astray. Mum had had to stand up to her.

Apart from that short time, the atmosphere was cheerful and kind and full of jokes. When it was time for the customers to leave and for the doors to be locked at the end of the day, one of the managers used to go quickly from floor to floor, calling out, 'Have you cleared your drawers, girls?'

Mum worked at Yeo's for seven happy years until 1931.

---

*   I have kept Mum's words even when they differ slightly from the correct text of songs or poems, an indication of how her memory stood up to the passing of many years.

Confirmation at Plympton St Mary's Church
November 1924

'Be faithful unto death':
    such easy words
When death is far away.
    White frocks for girls
With shoes to match;
    dark suits for boys,
With darns, and patched;
    the Bishop garbed
In purple robes.
    His text runs on –
'And I will give
    you then a crown
Of life.' And life's
    so troublesome
But fresh and green.
    How can it end?

Like this: a bed,
    a catheter,
A rattling breath,
    a gasp for air.

The words bore fruit –
    piled high, pressed down,
It overflows.
    How could he know,
That man – grey hair,
    a shepherd's crook
Blue eyes, shy smile?
    Yet in his voice
The ring of truth
    that stood the test
Of time, run out:
    the crown is hers.

2

'Dear Octopus'

BOTH OF MUM'S PARENTS had been in service.

On her mother's side of the family, the Alderseys, it had begun with Mum's grandfather and grandmother. By the 1840s they had been drawn to London to find work.

Young people were by then no longer needed in such numbers to work on the land, especially after the abolition of the Corn Laws and the fall in prices that followed the loss of the protection that they gave. Cereals gave way to cattle and sheep. The wages of farm labourers fell. London was growing quickly and on a great scale. Because of the fruits of the industrial revolution and of Great Britain's trade with her Empire and the rest of the world, the middle classes were growing richer. In the capital and in other big towns demand grew for domestic servants.

Like tens of thousands of others, Mum's grandparents found their way to London to earn their living. After a time there as domestic servants they moved back to their rural roots in Nottinghamshire. In 1866 Mum's mother, Agnes, was born. Agnes' father was by then working there as a gamekeeper on an estate. The Aldersey family continued to have a strong sense of belonging to the land. That feeling never left them or their descendants.

About twenty years later, in her turn, Agnes moved to London. She earned her living as a kitchen-maid and, with experience and training, as a cook.

For a while Agnes served the Prince and Princess of Wales in their household at Marlborough House. At that time her hair was jet-black and her fellow servants called her 'The Raven'. Once, running through the corridors of the building from the servants' hall to serve in the dining room, Agnes met the Prince. He stopped her and asked why she was running. She explained that the servants had little time to finish their own food before serving him and his guests at table. After that encounter the times of the meals were changed to give the servants time to eat properly before meals were served 'upstairs'.

After her adventures at Marlborough House, with visits to Sandringham with the Royal family at Christmas, Agnes went to work as head cook for a family in Putney. It was there that she met Henry, her future husband, serving as valet in the same house.

Henry was born in 1867. His family, the Jarrolds, gave him a much harsher start in life than Agnes' had given her. Afterwards, however, he was to find himself unusually blessed in his marriage and in the family that he and his wife would produce and cherish.

Henry's father, Elijah, had moved from Stowmarket in Suffolk to work as a builder's labourer in London in the 1860s. His wife, Emma, died in childbirth when she was only twenty-eight years old. Elijah became a heavy drinker and remarried. He sadistically bullied the children of his first marriage. He threw Henry out of the house when he was a boy of only seven.

Henry somehow found his way from London to York. He was brought up and educated there in a school for orphans run by a lady called Miss Milner. He remained devoted to her memory all his life. He went into service as a 'boots boy'. He did well. As a valet and later a butler in the next few years,

Henry sometimes travelled to Ireland and Scotland in the summer and to the South of France and Corfu in the winter. When she heard them as a young girl, Mum was fascinated by the tales of his journeys on the Continent with his 'gentleman's family'.

In 1892, eighteen years after he had rid himself of Henry and perhaps other children, Elijah met a terrible fate. *The Westminster and Pimlico News* of September the ninth reported:

'A Pimlico man's fatal fall.

'At St. George's Hospital Mr. Barnes held an inquest last Saturday with reference to the death of Elijah Jarrold, aged 50, a builder's labourer. Edward Edwards of 132, Pimlico road said that on Thursday week, the 25th ult., he was with the deceased, washing the front of 47, Park St., W, preparatory to painting. They were at the second floor window, and the deceased was standing on a board, one end of which was resting on an ordinary pair of steps in the room. He was holding onto the upper window sash, and was in the act of changing hands when he suddenly fell to the ground, a distance of about 20 feet. Notwithstanding fearful injuries, the man lingered till the 31st. A post mortem examination revealed that the base of the skull was fractured and the cause of death was shock from the injuries. The jury returned a verdict of "Accidental Death".'

Henry seems to have heard nothing of his father's death. He was already 25 years old. In later years Mum was the only person in his growing family to whom he spoke about his unhappy early years; even to her he said little.

In 1895, at the age of twenty-eight, Henry and Agnes married in London. With Mum's arrival in 1909, they completed their family of eight children – five sons and three daughters. During those fourteen years they were often on the move around England, in service with various families.

After service at Tehidy House in Cornwall, where Mum was born, the family moved to Plymouth. For two years Henry and Agnes kept a sweetshop there. It was unprofitable. According to Mum, her parents were too generous to many of the local children as well as their own.

In 1912 they moved to Plympton St Mary, five miles east of Plymouth. Henry returned to butlering, first for the Strode family at Newnham House, and afterwards for the families at Hemerdon House and Cann House, Tamerton Foliot.

The ten Jarrolds lived in a terraced house with three bedrooms at Number 12, Moorland View (later re-named and re-numbered as 24, Moorland Avenue). It is to this house that Mum's first memories relate. In 1922 the family moved from Moorland View to Number 7, Stone Barton. To mark their move and her thirteenth birthday, Mum planted a lilac tree beside the front door.

A friendly community grew up at Stone Barton. Each house was home to a family big by today's standards. It was a world, and a class, without the scars of divorce. Gardens were gardens, not concreted over for cars. Children could play safely outside all day. They grew up together, forging links that were to last eighty years in some cases. This was so for Mum. It gave her great joy.

Mum's parents were pillars of this society, the sort of people to whom others turned for comfort and help. Perhaps this was because of their experience, wider than that of many of the locals; perhaps it was because they were older than many of the other heads of households; but almost certainly their character, especially Agnes', is an important part of the explanation.

Henry was about 5'9" tall. He was of stocky build and had a sallow complexion. His bearing was erect and he carried himself well, impressive as a butler, requiring and surely receiving obedience from all the servants below stairs. His own family had something of that attitude towards him. He was a smart man and always dressed formally, with a collar and tie. In his retirement he looked much as he had during his many years as a valet and butler.

Henry had a serious and sometimes solemn face. He could be stern. His voice was deep, with a Midlands accent, and he used it dramatically. He ruled the family firmly. Everyone bowed to his way of doing things. Even at the end, when he was often in bed because of heart tremors, he directed the family's life decisively. Everything he did was tinged with a certain sense of theatre. *'I'm going,'* he would say if he felt a palpitation and all the family would gather around his bed.

For all this, Henry was loved by his family and respected with affection by the neighbours. He was a benign version of his cruel father, perhaps civilised and redeemed by his exceptional wife.

Agnes was a little taller than her husband. She was an imposing person, with a presence. Everyone spoke of *'Mrs Jarrold'* in a respectful tone of voice that seemed to acknowledge special qualities. As long as there were people in Plympton who remembered her, for fifty years after her death, this tone of voice could be heard when people spoke of her.

Agnes' own voice was resonant, with a Midlands accent and a decisive note. Her face was oval and rather thin, with a pale complexion and dark grey eyes. The expression on her face was peaceful and calm, and often serious. Her straight hair, now white, she wore in a bun. She had an erect, Victorian posture and always bore herself well. Her walk remained brisk until her last years. Then she began to slow down and to hobble a little, but she never made use of a stick.

Agnes was simple in her tastes and manner, and rather austere except on special occasions. When she was making mince-pies at Christmas, singing hymns and carols, she sipped from a glass of stout on the corner of the kitchen range. Above all, she was kind and considerate. The only thing that mattered to her was the well-being of the family.

The Jarrold family used to gather to sing around the piano in the little back drawing-room, as they called it, where Mum played for them. They were proud of their piano, engraved in gilt letters, *'W. Daneman and Company, London, 1883'*. When Henry was butler at Tehidy House, his sons had loaded it on to a donkey cart at William Chandler's 'Piano and Music Salon' in Redruth and brought it the three or four miles to their tied cottage. In those days Agnes had also played the piano. In due course she bequeathed it to Mum.

Agnes was a beloved matriarch, in charge of the day-to-day running of the house. She, rather than Henry, was the brains of their long and successful partnership.

'She was endowed with a great capacity for loving people. She was marvellous. She gave everything to them,' my cousin John told me. 'Grandmother and grandfather generated a very happy, lively atmosphere, with never any strain except for his turns of ill health.'

And Mum told me, *'Father was always smartly dressed and always raised his hat to a lady.* "Without manners, there is nothing," *he used to say. He was very steadfast, stern and caring, a good man. My mother used to say how strong he was. They were both like that:*

> "It's easy enough to be pleasant
> When life flows along like a song,
> But the one worthwhile
> Is the one who can smile
> When everything goes dead wrong.
> The test of the heart is trouble,
> And it always comes with the years;
> But the one who is worth
> The salt of the earth
> Is the one who can smile through tears".'

One August Bank Holiday when Mum was in her seventies, Judy and I sat with her under Dad's pear tree in her little back-garden. We listened to *Dear Octopus* by Dodie Smith, one of Mum's favourite plays. It is the story of a family – 'that dear octopus' – under pressure in various ways, but somehow managing to hold together. The play ends with a speech delivered by the father of the clan at a family party.

As Mum wrote of another of her favourite plays, '*It is family life as it really was a few years ago, people really standing up for each other.*'

Mum, too, believed in the saving power of the family's embrace. When all else failed, the family, if you nurtured it and people respected each other, would not let you down.

3

'Tea at Gunters'

IN THE SUMMER of 1922 Wally reached his sixteenth birthday and left Plymouth Corporation Grammar School. He passed his school certificate with flying colours and received 'matriculation exemption' for university, but there was no question of his taking that up. With his mother he visited various offices in Plymouth and she helped him get a job. He joined the Great Western Railway and started work as a booking-clerk.

'Wal was nervous and mother gave him confidence,' Mum told me.

Wally spent all his working life on the railways, first the G.W.R. and later British Railways after nationalisation. He was not at all well paid at first. In his family only he and perhaps, in those days, Jack held strong political views. In a small way Wally became involved in the turmoil of the General Strike in May 1926. Perhaps Jack influenced him.

Railwaymen, dockers, and bus drivers went on strike in support of the coal miners, who had rejected a cut in their wages and had been locked out of the mines by the pit owners. Wally joined in. The strike began to collapse after a few days. On the twelfth of May the Trade Union Congress backed down and called it off. The miners remained on strike until mid-November, when they could do nothing but accept the wage cuts, the prospect of which had provoked the strike in the first place.

Wally was sacked. His dismissal was a terrible blow for him, so young and at the beginning of his career, and for his parents. They had staked so much on his education and were distraught. His mother put on her smart black dress, hat and coat, and went to Flete House to call on Lord Mildmay. He was a director of the company, and he agreed to take Wally back onto the payroll.

Mum told me that his actions in the strike had deeply upset their mother: *'She wasn't going to let Wally down, but it wasn't easy for her to bow the knee and she came home and cried, although she had succeeded.'*

Wally grieved that his mother had had to do this for him. He believed that he had played a part in humiliating her. His political views softened as time passed. He never spoke of what had happened in 1926.

Much later, Wally and Mum sometimes disagreed about politics at election-time. One spring afternoon in his late seventies, he and his wife, Audrey, took Mum for a drive in the Devon lanes. A general election campaign was in progress.

Mum always feared the sour debate, often personal, that blew up between party politicians during elections. Mum was a Conservative voter, but not dogmatic about politics, which she did not like at the most peaceful of times. She always sympathised with the futile efforts and inevitable defeat of the Labour candidate in the local elections. *'I told him,* "You haven't got a hope here in Plympton, Mr Jakeway. We all vote Conservative," *and he looked so crestfallen that I gave him a cup of tea.'*

On the drive Wally said to Mum that anyone who thought of himself as a Christian and did not vote socialist was a hypocrite. *'Poor Audrey was in the middle, and I told Wal,* "Well, I'm a hypocrite, Wal." *Anyhow, we ended up joking ... It will be lovely when the election is over and people stop running each other down.'*

Their political differences did not erode their affection for each other or prevent their sharing a far greater truth. At around the same time, Mum wrote, '*I knelt with Wal at the Holy Communion table on Sunday and was at evensong with him and Audrey in the evening ... I do not think that another brother and sister were at Communion ... I am sure that Wal felt this also.*'

They shared many jokes. During the Second World War Wally was the manager of a strategic railway junction and signal box near Plymouth. He had many staff in his charge. The responsibility worried him, but sometimes also lightened life. One young woman, the daughter of a formidable mother and mild-mannered father, came to work one morning with the words, 'Daddy's left home – and he's taken the sweet coupons with him'. 'Daddy' had made good his escape, with the most prized page of the ration book. His daughter's words lived on through the decades for Mum and Wally. Humour and faith kept them good friends.

Although Mum was, in her words, '*timid and anxious*' when she started work in 1924, she had already begun to spread her wings. With one of her school friends, Millie Hayes, she went with two young men, riding pillion on a motorcycle, to the seaside for the day. '*I was nearly blown away by the wind, and then got cold swimming there.*'

In late 1926 or early 1927, she and Wally visited their relations in London. It was the first time that she had stayed away from her home. Perhaps their parents arranged for them to go there for a holiday to help Wally put the events of the strike behind him.

For two weeks Mum and Wally stayed with their Uncle Jack, their mother's brother, and his wife, Auntie Nellie. Uncle Jack and Auntie Nellie lived in a flat on the third floor at 9, Balderton Buildings, Brown Hart Gardens, a Peabody Trust building near Oxford Street. Jack was now the mainstay of the Aldersey family, eight brothers and sisters whom he worked hard to keep in touch with one other.

It took Mum a while to overcome her homesickness. 'Will she ever stop crying?' Uncle Jack demanded. 'She'll have to go home if she doesn't stop "whinnicking". I can't bear it any longer.'

Mum stopped. She was enjoying the thrill of being in the capital of the greatest empire the world had ever seen too much to risk being sent home early. Besides, Auntie Nellie was a wonderful cook.

Uncle Jack had gone into service as a young man as a valet and butler. By 1927 he had been working for some time at Gunters, the well-known Mayfair tea-room in Curzon Street. He welcomed the customers and assisted them with their hats and coats. Knowing him well, they gave him generous tips. He had a distinguished, courteous manner and a gallant bearing. To her pride, Uncle Jack introduced Mum to his regular customers as 'my niece, up from the country'. The staff there regarded him as their father or elder brother. He and Nellie could have no children of their own.

At the end of each day Uncle Jack used to take home a few of the tiny sandwiches and exquisite cakes that had been left over. Mum's memories of these treats caused her to dream of that visit to London whenever Gunters was mentioned. In her seventies, by when the teashop had long since ceased to exist, she relished a play on the radio, *Tea at Gunters*. Perhaps, like Auntie Nellie's cooking, the sandwiches and cakes finally made Mum feel at home in London, reminding her of taking tea after work with her mother at Goodbody Matthews in Plymouth.

Mum and Wally explored London. They ventured onto the Serpentine in Hyde Park in a rowing-boat. Wally was infuriated when Mum could not give him clear directions as he rowed; she circled in one spot or zigzagged across the lake. But Wally was proud of his sister. With her good looks and smart clothes, a new suit with a hat and shoes bought specially for the visit, she made a good impression on everyone that they met. 'You're the best-looking girl in London,' he said to her. '*It was the suit that Jimmy Common made for me that made me look like that,'* Mum told me. *'He was a wonderful tailor.'* Mr Common, the Plympton tailor, was an old friend of their family.

At the end of their holiday they went shopping in Oxford Street and the Edgware Road. They bought seven parcels, presents for their aunt and uncle, and others to take back to Plympton. As they went back to the flat, exhausted from walking the length of Edgware Road, Mum noticed that one of her parcels was missing. She had twisted the string of each one around one of her fingers and somehow had dropped one.

Wally was furious. The missing present was a pair of red slippers for Auntie Nellie. They retraced their steps and bought another pair. They made their way back to Balderton Buildings for their last evening together. Auntie Nellie gave Mum a gold bangle bracelet. A few years later, when her mother's eyesight grew weak, Mum sold it and used the money to buy her a hymn-book with large print, which her mother used every Sunday. Uncle Jack gave Mum a smart top-coat, made by his tailor.

The next day Uncle Jack and Auntie Nellie saw Wally and Mum off at Paddington station. Mum had become their favourite niece.

In the 1970s, fifty years after that fortnight in London, Judy and I took Mum to Brown Hart Gardens. Auntie Nellie, and after her Uncle Jack, had died long ago. Auntie Alice, Jack's second wife, was still living there as her life in its turn was drawing to its end.

It was the August bank holiday. In the 'Seventies most of the shops in Oxford Street used to close for the holiday. The centre of London was deserted and quiet. We found plenty of parking space for our car, not far from the Ukrainian Uniate cathedral, and walked to Balderton Flats, as the block had been renamed. We met no one on the way there. It was as if, for a moment, we were in the past, and Wally and Mum, still young people of twenty and seventeen years, might come around the corner, on their way back from the Serpentine or from their shopping adventure in the Edgware Road, with their parcels.

The flats have been done up since our visits there in the 1970s, but at that time they were much as they had been in the 1920s. There was still an outside stone staircase in the inner courtyard, half exposed to the weather, to take us up to Auntie Alice's flat. The lavatory belonging to each little flat was set apart from it, across the landing on the stair-well. This curious arrangement was presumably designed by the Peabody Trust in the interest of hygiene, but it could confuse visitors. On the first morning of their stay in 1926, Mum had opened the wrong door and, to her consternation and embarrassment, had found a stranger sitting on the seat in what she had taken to be her uncle and aunt's lavatory. Mum began to explain at length who she was and how she made the mistake, while the neighbour urgently encouraged her to close the door and leave.

Auntie Alice was a rather frail lady by this time, slight in build, with a pale, round face, glasses, and a pointed nose. She was cheerful and bright, and kept the flat beautifully clean and tidy, with many mementoes of Uncle Jack, and of Auntie Nellie's days. Auntie Alice was as fond of Mum as had been Auntie Nellie. She gave us a wonderful plum tart for tea. We washed up together in her little kitchen. Auntie Alice and Mum reminisced about Uncle Jack and the Aldersey family, and Auntie Alice was interested in us and our doings.

When she got home, Mum wrote to us. '*I had a nice letter from Auntie Alice this morning. She said how much she enjoyed seeing us. She would like to come down to Devon but doesn't relish the journey… It was so nice of you to take me to see her. I hope that she will enjoy her holiday in Eastbourne.*'

Over the next couple of years Judy and I took Mum to visit her twice more, the last time not long before Auntie Alice's final illness. Mum told me that her niece had written to tell her, '*She is quite happy but living in a little world of her own.*'

Auntie Alice died in the early spring of 1980. In her will she left Mum £500. Mum was overwhelmed by this generous and kind act, the only occasion when she received any money in a will, except for £8 from her mother, and, of course, everything that Dad had left. '*I have not got used to it yet,*' she told me. '*I never wanted to receive money through anyone dying. It was good that you took me to see her.*'

Mum used the money to renew the electrical wiring in her house, just in time for Christmas that year. '*It is chaos here. The house is in an awful muddle, beds on top of one other. I suppose it will soon be over. I feel the house is not my own this morning.*' She was always grateful to Auntie Alice. '*I do so love Number 10 Moorland Road, as did Dad.*'

After returning to Devon from London, Mum went back to work at Yeo's. Her life in the late 1920s and early 1930s revolved around home and work, her family and her colleagues. She continued to read quite widely.

The family went on a few special outings. When Castle Drogo, near Drewsteignton, was given to the National Trust by the Drewe family in 1974, Mum told me, '*I saw it when I was about eighteen, out for a drive with my Mum and Dad, Arthur, Wal and with Fred driving a taxi we hired for the outing. I thought it was lovely and the scenery superb... I hope we can go there again one day now that it will be open to the public.*'

At school Mum had made a good friend, Marietta Burgess. Marietta was a lively girl, with a turned-up nose. She loved to visit Mum's house, and used to sit on the kitchen table, with her feet on a chair, playing her ukulele. '*Mother loved her because she made her laugh,*' Mum told me.

The Burgesses lived in a detached house at the end of Stone Barton, opposite Treverbyn, the grand offices of the Rural District Council. Plympton St Mary was believed to be the most extensive Rural District in England at that time. The red-brick building, with its fine granite gateway, was demolished in the 1990s.

Mr Burgess was a senior officer in the R.D.C. His steady rise at work – eventually he became Clerk to the Council – put him in a small, professional class in Plympton, unlike the fathers of Mum's other friends. He ran a motor-car.

The Burgesses used to take Mum along on outings in their Morris Cowley as company for Marietta. Wearing hats with wide brims and veils to protect their hair, the two girls used to sit in the open dicky seat, with the hood down. The Burgesses had a family link with North Devon and once in summer they took Mum to Combe Martin. They gave her many good outings.

Marietta became a pretty young woman.

'I was jealous of her when she got a boy friend,' Mum said. *'She was soon engaged to be married and made a good match. I gave her a wedding present, and she was a lovely bride, but she didn't invite me to the wedding.*

'When Mr Burgess came in to see Mother in the kitchen afterwards I was there. He must have realised that I was a bit sad and disappointed.

' "I hoped you wouldn't feel like that, Grace," *he said.* "You know what they are like. It's all gloss and veneer." *Mr Burgess was ashamed of the way they treated me.'*

Marietta's turned-up nose proved to be symbolic. She had inherited, or adapted her ways to, her mother's snobbery. Mr Burgess' success did not change him. He continued to visit the kitchen at Number 7, and to give Mum some of the strawberries that he grew in his back garden, which she loved. She admired the way in which he established primroses and meadowsweet in the hedge in front of his house.

One afternoon, sixty years later, I am sitting beside Mum's bed in Ward 12. It is the quiet period when the nurses and helpers have collected all the plates and cutlery. Some of the patients have nodded off. I have just given Mum some early Cornish strawberries. Perhaps they remind her of her happy memories of the times when Mr Burgess brought her family some of his.

'*He was a nice man,*' she says. But her mind moves on to the story of Marietta's wedding, and she reminds me of it.

After a long pause, she adds, '*I was no worse than Marietta.*'

Mum absorbed the pain of that '*bit of snobbery*' and rejection into herself. She could not imagine that she would reject anyone for such a reason. She had thought, at the time, that what had happened must show that Marietta and her mother felt that there was something inferior about her in a deeper way.

Something entered Mum's heart (perhaps it was always there) that made her feel unworthy, unaccepted and, for some reason she could not fathom, unacceptable. Only now, at the end of her life, does Mum come to realise and say openly that she does not believe that any longer. '*Marietta felt that they were a step higher than us. It was sad, really. I was a bit hurt. I felt as good as anybody. I was always proud of mother. I thought she was wonderful.*

'*A lot of us are nobodies and go through the world feeling that, and getting no recognition. Some people are noticed all the time and they don't realise that other people are sad because they are unappreciated and unnoticed. In a way, it's bad to be noticed too much, because then you expect it all the time, and it's painful if it doesn't arrive. There's a great gap there, and others don't know what you're missing...*

'*I mustn't snivel. When life is at its healthiest, make the most of it. Don't take it for granted. Mother used to say* "Life is a burden – bear it. Life is a crown of thorns – wear it." *It's hard, but most of it is lovely. Don't be frightened... There is always someone to pick up the pieces; it's strange but there always is.*'

4

'The test
of the heart
is trouble'

IN OCTOBER 1930 Mum's family held a party for her twenty-first birthday. Her parents gave her a gold wristwatch, and her friend Iris Williams stayed the night after the party. She gave Mum a pink nightdress and a dressing-gown. They were good friends, and Mum hoped that Iris would marry her brother Jack.

Not long after that, in the early 'Thirties, Mum gave up her job at Yeo's. She always regretted doing so. She had been doing well and enjoyed the work.

'I should have done what I wanted, but one of the other girls kept saying that she hated the work, and she influenced me. I should have listened to what Lily Coombes said, but that other one turned me against it. I liked working there, but I gave in my notice. Mother wanted me to stay at Yeo's.'

So, in her early twenties, Mum settled into a life of helping her mother to keep house for her father and her four unmarried brothers. Both her sisters and one of her brothers were already married. By now her mother really needed her help.

After bearing eight children Agnes had suffered a miscarriage. For twenty-five years she had moved with Henry and their growing family from house to house around the country wherever his work had taken him, from London to Northamptonshire, the North Riding of Yorkshire, Worcestershire and Cornwall. She had lived through the Great War of 1914 to 1918, constantly fearing for her two eldest sons, in the Royal Artillery and the Cavalry. She had lived solely for her family, to make them happy. She had succeeded, and she was exhausted. By now sixty-four years old, she was perhaps in her late middle-age by the standards eighty years later but, in her day, she was elderly.

Mum's father had been a semi-invalid for several years. From his middle age Henry suffered from a weak heart. For a while, at the start of the Great War, he worked in the Royal Naval dockyard at Devonport. He was by then in his late forties, and his health broke down. 'You can't make a race-horse do the work of a cart-horse, Mrs Jarrold,' Dr Stamp told Agnes when he visited them at Number 7 in his pony and trap, wearing his formal suit and top-hat.

Henry was able to go back to work as a butler after a time but he suffered a heart attack in 1923, when he was fifty-five years old.

One sunny day in the early spring of that year during the Easter holidays he had walked home from work at Tamerton through Plymbridge woods, which had been white with snow-drops a few weeks earlier. Agnes and Mum were in the midst of washing up the midday dinner dishes. Mum was thirteen at the time. She was in her last year at school.

Soon after he arrived home Henry collapsed over the kitchen table.

With Mum's help, Agnes made a fire for Henry in their bedroom and they settled him there. For a while his life was in the balance. Dr Stamp told Agnes that Henry might die at any moment and, in any case, had not many months to live. 'We'll see about that,' Agnes said.

Henry's health improved gradually. Although he had to retire, he quite soon re-asserted himself as head of the household. Agnes gave him a healthy diet with no red meat, fat or cream. She cosseted him, and encouraged him to take regular, steady exercise. She was determined to keep Henry alive and well. His heart-trouble often made his sallow, square face and his bald head flush a deep red. *'Mother treated him like gold dust,'* Mum told me.

Henry had enjoyed his work as a butler. The years of enforced retirement were not easy for him or Agnes.

In earlier years they had taken their children to the panto-mime each Christmas at the Palace Theatre in Plymouth. One year there was a song which Agnes and Mum used to sing to make light of the unstinting care that they now had to give Henry:

> *'I wake him in the morning when the clock strikes eight;*
> *I'm always punctual, never, never late:*
> *A nice cup of tea and a little round of toast,*
> The Sporting Life *and* The Winning Post.
> *I make him nice and comfy*
> *Then I toddle off to work –*
> *For I'm only doing what a woman should do,*
> *For he's only a working man.'*

Each morning Mum took her father tea in bed, followed a little later by his shaving water in a gunmetal mug and a bowl of water to be put on his wash-stand. Henry got up and vigorously splashed himself with a flannel. He spent the rest of the morning resting upstairs in the bedroom, with its peaceful green and cream wallpaper, decorated with rose patterns.

In the afternoon he took his 'constitutional' in the lanes around Plympton, leaning on his walking stick with its silver handle and making a point of picking up any buttons which he noticed in the road. He kept these in an old Kruschen Salts bottle, together with a few florin pieces that he secretly hoarded against the day when Agnes would need a little extra money. When he saw Agnes looking worried, Henry quietly went upstairs and proudly produced that bottle to save the day.

Sometimes he bet threepence (3d, now 1p) each way on a horse. If he lost he retired upstairs to lick his wounds. *'He'd say that he had a headache,'* Mum said, *'But no one said, "Poor old Dad's got a headache," just "Poor old Dad, he's lost on the races again." '*

This peaceful routine gave him another sixteen years' life.

Mum's family was poor; nothing like as hard-pressed as Dad and his sisters had been during their childhood and youth in Cornwall, but poor nevertheless. She told me that when she was helping her mother keep house in the 1920s and 1930s and they were dusting and sweeping together, she used to take up a piece of coconut matting in the sitting-room in order to clean the floor. There was no carpet. There never was, except for special occasions when they borrowed one. Many families lived like that in those days.

'In the morning I would clean the house and go to the shops at Colebrook. In the afternoon I would sometimes go for a ride on my Raleigh bike to Lee Moor and free-wheel back down the lanes from the edge of Dartmoor. Then I would cut dozens of thin slices of bread and butter for tea. The seven of us would sit down around the dining-table together, with a huge plate of bread and butter at each end of the table, and one of Mother's rabbit pies if we were lucky.'

Once a week in the 'Thirties Mum and her mother continued to go to Plymouth on the 5.09 pm train for tea at Goodbody Matthews, and a film at the Gaumont or Andrews cinema. They would return on the 9.20 train. It was the highlight of their week.

On Sundays they would go to the service at St Mary's church. They also listened to services on the radio. *'It's strange that you should be going to St Michael's, Chester Square, in London,'* Mum commented to us in 1985 or 1986, when we went to that church on Sunday evenings for a specially contemplative and encouraging service at a time of great need. *'My Mum and Dad and I regularly listened to the service from there. There was a truly wonderful preacher. I wish I could remember his name.'* *

Perhaps Agnes and Henry made their home too happy and their children too welcome. Most of them were rather slow to get married and to begin their own families.

'We were always jolly in our house. Mother always had her hands in flour, cooking for us hungry ones… We always seemed to have a nice meal put before us. My mother knew the way to cook a meal. My brothers went rabbiting, and no one could roast rabbits like Mother. She made bread and saffron cake in the Cornish range. We all loved saffron cake.'

Henry's sons, especially Arthur, were a great comfort to him, but he had worried about his two eldest daughters and their prospects of marriage. He also worried about Mum, so much younger than the other two.

Harry, the eldest son, married Maggie in February 1920. He was twenty-four years old and his work on the G.W.R. took him from time to time to South Wales. When he proposed to Maggie his parents feared that he was seeking a quick escape from all the horrors that he had seen and heard on the Western Front. She was six years younger than Harry and from a background unlike his own, in one of the industrial villages of the mining valleys.

Over the years Harry and Maggie lived in several of the towns linked by the railway. Finally they settled at Laira, then a separate village on the main road, midway between Plymouth and Plympton, famous among railwaymen as the setting for a magnificent shunting and marshalling yard on the wide, flat ground on the western side of the Plym estuary.

Harry and Maggie, and in time their children, attended St Mary's church in Laira. He was a member of the choir for

*   He was Canon Wallace Harold Elliott, Vicar of St Michael's from 1930 to 1941.

almost fifty years, making good use of his resonant and affecting baritone voice. He performed music-hall songs at church events. Sporting the top-hat that his father had occasionally used in his work, Harry would dress up in white tie and tails and deliver such songs as 'Burlington Bertie from Bow'. He did this with an insouciance, innocence and geniality that seemed to combine, in harmony, the qualities that he had inherited from both his extrovert, histrionic father and his impressive, calm mother.

Harry was fourteen years older than Mum and he always looked on her as a baby. *'He used to call me "Nacy Noo" and the rest of them picked that up from him.'*

Whatever fears his parents had felt, Harry's marriage proved exceptionally happy. He and Maggie had produced three children – John, Agnes and Cyril – and had enjoyed fifty-five years together when he died in 1975. A new Bible lectern was dedicated at St Mary's in memory of him.

Edie was the next to marry. She was twenty-four when she settled down with her husband, Len, in April 1921. Len was also a railwayman.

'Edie was twelve years older than me, and had pushed me in the pram around Plympton. I was her bridesmaid. She was a wonderful needlewoman. She crocheted all her sheets and towels for her bottom drawer. She was very smart, never without a hat. She had worked in service at a big house on The Hoe in Plymouth before marrying Len.'

Edie and Len had three children, Joan, Gerald and Mavis. Edie died in 1953.

Jack, three years younger than Edie, never married. He had been fifteen years old when the Great War broke out, and had joined the Army a year or two later to serve in the Cavalry. The experience affected him more deeply than Harry.

'Jack was a very gentle man,' Mum told me. *'Quite the opposite of warlike ... It must have been awful for him to kill people who had never done him a bit of harm ...*

'He knew that he was the best-looking of my brothers, but Iris Williams wouldn't marry him and he never loved anyone else ...

'*Mr Williams had a good job as the Paymaster in the Royal Navy at Devonport dockyard. Mrs Williams liked Jack but Iris's father feared that Jack would not be able to provide for her properly… I wish Iris had married Jack. He would have loved to have had a family and children. Iris was the only girl he loved, but she didn't stick to him, because of what her father said.*'

It was Jack who, to his horror, foresaw most clearly the coming of war in the 'Thirties. In late 1938 or early 1939, he pressed his brother George to help him dig an air-raid shelter in the front garden at Number 7. Passers-by at Stone Barton made fun of them for what they were doing.

When war broke out, Jack again served loyally, this time in the Royal Observer Corps. His unit was based on the peak of Dorsmouth Rock, a hill which rises to three hundred and thirteen feet to the south of Plympton. From there he identified the German aircraft as they made their descent to attack Plymouth, and watched the fires that destroyed the old city in the Blitz.

In war and peace Jack found comfort when he went for long walks in the woods at dawn or dusk with his many dogs. He did jobbing gardening to earn his living, and enjoyed a quiet life at home. He knew all the farmers and country-folk far and wide and he helped them deal with foxes and badgers that were causing problems for their stock. In the depths of winter, when the farmers were cut off by snow on Dartmoor, Jack would trek miles to take them supplies.

Jack inherited the skills of a gamekeeper from his mother's line. He was a wonderful shot. He used to roam the fields and woods and bring home rabbits and pigeons for the table. He had a tender heart. His terriers were well-trained working dogs, but when he lost one of them down the shaft of the disused wolfram mine at Hemerdon he could not rest. He returned to the site day after day until finally he heard its faint cries. He remained upset for days that the only way to save the dog from dying from lack of water was to shoot it at the bottom of the shaft.

As a child, I felt that there was something hidden and wounded in Jack behind his deep, clear blue eyes. He was quietly spoken and kind. In later years, when occasionally we met on walks, he was interested in talking about the countryside. Late in his life he still used to go to the woods with his dogs in the early spring to listen to the dawn chorus.

'He was a very good man,' Mum told me.

Hilda married Fred in July 1927. She was twenty-seven. Fred was well known in the village as a keen footballer and boxer. He came from Plympton St Maurice. Hilda and Fred, who was a couple of years younger, met at school. They worked together when Hilda was a housemaid and Fred the driver at Castle Cot, Miss Tritton's house. Miss Tritton was the niece of General Sir Redvers Buller V.C., famous for leading the force that relieved Ladysmith in 1900 in the Boer War.

'When Miss Tritton married the curate at St Maurice's church, they went on honeymoon to a house on Dartmoor, near Chagford. Fred drove them there in her motorcar and Hilda went to take care of them.

'My friend Winnie Boulden and I were Hilda's bridesmaids.'

The marriage lasted happily for forty-eight years until Hilda's death in 1975. Their son, John, also married happily and gave Hilda and Fred three grandsons.

George was two years younger than Hilda. He had a generous spirit, quick wits and good looks. Unlike the rest of the family he was feckless and sometimes irresponsible. Perhaps his charm was a curse. He had been too young to serve in the Great War. He did not marry.

Like almost everyone else, Mum found it difficult to disapprove of his erratic, thoughtless ways for long. She pitied him for being unable to settle down. *'George was different,'* she told me. *'He wasn't close friends with any of us; he was the odd one out.'*

☯

For eight years after Hilda's wedding in 1927 Mum lived at Number 7 with her parents, Jack, George and her two youngest brothers Arthur and Wally. From 1931 she was at home, full-time, helping her mother keep house for the five men-folk.

The pattern at Number 7 was broken in the mid-1930s when, within a year of each other, Wally and Arthur moved away.

Wally was doing well on the railway. Like others in the family, he found in it a responsible and worthwhile job. It was not yet fifty years since Edward King, the saintly Bishop of Lincoln, whose broad diocese was crossed by many main lines, had praised the railway companies and their workers for the sense of discipline, cooperation and service shown in their work and way of life; a network that held together cities, towns and villages, industry, farms and fishing fleets, and helped give the country a strong identity and purpose. The nostalgia felt by some men for steam trains may not just be a matter of the smell of smoke and steam and the hiss of engines.

In 1934 Wally met Audrey, a young nurse and nanny. He used to see her as he made his way home in the afternoon from the railway station to Number 7. Audrey would be pushing a pram, or walking with the other children for whom she was caring, often wearing a pink linen dress, with her silky black hair cascading over a white collar. She was working for a family who lived in Boringdon Villas, a row of impressive Victorian houses built of the local limestone. As they got to know each other, Wally used to whistle a love song, 'They call her Mary', below her attic window, whenever he walked past her house.

Later that year Wally asked Mum for her advice. Should he propose marriage to Audrey or Doris Blake? Mum advised him, *'Doris has got lovely legs, but Audrey has beautiful hair and is very smart.'* Mum always loved Audrey. Wally took Mum's advice.

So, in October 1935, less than ten years after the General Strike that had caused him such trouble, Wally and Audrey married, with Arthur as Wally's best man. Wally and Audrey set up home in a newly-built house on the far side of Plymouth, at Pemros Road, about six miles away from Number 7, not far from the River Tamar and the Royal Navy's dockyard at Devonport.

In the summer of 1936 it was Wally's turn to act as Arthur's best man.

Arthur was two years older than Wally. The whole family held Arthur in special affection and respect. Arthur did much to keep his brothers and sisters together, supporting each other and their parents. He worked hard to keep George on the rails and helped him to find a decent job. Once as he handed George half a crown (25p) to help him out when he had fallen into debt, he looked at him with concern and just said, 'Waster.' *12½*

'A word from Arthur and he felt very small,' Mum said. *'Arthur did a lot for George. He helped him get a better job in one of his fruit and vegetable shops in Plymouth. He had been working at the hot china clay kilns at Lee Moor. The heat and steam there were damaging George's poor legs so much.'*

Arthur married Edna in June 1936.

'I remember seeing Edna for the first time in Colebrook when she was waiting for Arthur at the flower shop and nursery where Arthur was working,' Mum told me. *'She was about the same age as me. You would have liked her.*

'Arthur was a "belonger", like me. He used to go to eight o'clock Holy Communion and evensong at St Mary's. We all loved him. How much he used to help us all. He always made Father laugh.

'I went to tea with Arthur and Edna quite soon after they were married, at their new house at Number 12, Westways at Hooe. It was a Wednesday afternoon, and I cut the bread and butter. Edna's mother, Mrs. Sherrell, made a sponge-cake. She was a farmer's wife and a wonderful cook. Arthur and Edna eventually had five flower, fruit and vegetable shops in Plymouth. They were all bombed out in the Blitz.'

Arthur and Edna's marriage was tragically short.

As a boy, Arthur had hurt himself badly in an accident when he and his brothers were playing at the railway station. He slipped down between the platform and a stationary train. The fall bruised his back. Wishing not to worry his parents he did not tell them about it. Not long after his marriage, this wound reappeared and it became infected with tuberculosis. It ended a happy marriage and a generous, successful life. Arthur and

Edna had only two and a half years together. They were beginning to make a great success of their business. Arthur died on Boxing Day 1938.

The death certificate read, *'Heart failure. Endocarditis. Pulmonary abscess. Dr H.W. Thomas, MRCP.'*

The loss of her dearest brother, coming so early in his promising life, haunted Mum for the rest of her days. He was only thirty-four years old.

Of the eight children in the family, Arthur and Mum were the two most alike in character and, in affection, the closest to each other. Arthur had constantly sustained Mum with his moral support. He was a happy, kind man, full of fun and always thoughtful. He had a buoyant, jolly outlook, and an infectious guffaw of a laugh.

'Harry's wife, Maggie was very loving and motherly to me,' Mum told me. *'She made me a black dress so that I could mourn Arthur properly.'*

Edna remarried during the Second World War. For the rest of her life, she arranged for flowers to be placed on Arthur's grave at Christmas. Even after her death in 1979 there would be a wreath delivered on the instructions that Edna made in her will. The sight of the flowers there each year, in frosty sunshine or in Devon mist, always touched Mum's heart and caused her to shed some tears as she stood in silence at his grave, not far from where Arthur and Edna had lived together for such a short time.

One day in Ward 12, stirring herself from deep thought, Mum smiled and said to me, *'I was afraid that I'd forgotten Arthur's face, but I haven't.*

'People came all the way from the Channel Islands for his funeral, because of all the flowers grown there that he and Edna had sold.

'It's because he died so young and you never know what is going to happen to anyone that I am so keen on people being nice to each other. You never know what you are doing to people...

'Arthur was sensible and saved money. He was generous to people in need. He didn't tell anyone about it, and we found out after his death. Miss Mewton who lived in a tiny house in Ridgeway didn't have much money. She was a lovely lady and she told us that Arthur had given her five shillings. He bought Mother and Father a lovely suite of furniture for Number 7...'

After a pause, Mum added:

'It's been a lovely life, a very good life...

'I didn't much like being thirty, but everything was fine later.'

And only now does the penny drop for me that it was of this period, just after Wally had married Audrey, and Arthur had married Edna, that Mum spoke least often. In the years until 1938, she had been able to look forward to Arthur's daily visits to Number 7.

Every day, after working at their shop nearby in Colebrook, on his way home to Edna, five miles away at Hooe, he would call on his family. Often he took them a small treat, a quarter of clotted cream or some flowers or fruit. To the end of her life Mum's eyes would light up when she told me of these visits.

With his death, everything changed. Mum lost much of the warmth and cosiness that she craved all her life. She was twenty-nine.

Towards the end of the Indian summer of 1939 Henry arrived home for tea after an unusually long walk. He had gone to visit the last big house where he had served as butler, at Tamerton Foliot.

At the front gate he congratulated Jack and George on the progress they were making with the air-raid shelter in the front garden.

Mum greeted her father at the front door, as usual. She had already sliced the bread for his tea. The kettle was bubbling on the range. The teapot was warming. As Mum took her father's Homburg hat and walking stick from him, he fell dead in her arms. It was the eve of her birthday.

Had he been able to plan his massive stroke, Henry could not, in his histrionic imagination, have devised and carried off a more dramatic death scene. He died instantly. His death was hastened by the despair and anxiety that he and Agnes felt because of the second war with Germany in their lifetime.

He was greatly missed.

Agnes lived on for nearly four years.

In July 1943 during the renewed blitz of Plymouth, she decided to sit outside in the garden one night and watch the flames rising high into the sky from the great fires as the bombs fell on the city. The heat in the stuffy shelter had made her feel unwell, and she did not want to stay inside. She was hit by the blast from a bomb dropped by a German bomber as it sped eastwards, making its getaway.

Agnes took to her bed and died a few days later, surrounded by her children.

It was after the loss of her parents, two broken engagements, and many traumas in the War, that everything changed for Mum. On the fourth of December 1944 she met Dad when he was on leave from the Indian Army. They married twelve days later. She was happy.

Their happiness together, joy and woe, was to last twenty-eight years.*

In 1972 Dad died. He had been ill from Huntington's disease for many years. He died a year after I had married Judy. Because of his illness, by then severe, Judy never met Dad. It is her great regret. In Mum's words, '*Dad would have loved Judy.*'

---

* The story of those years does not belong here. I have done my best to tell it in *Stranger on the Shore*, published by Shepheard-Walwyn, 2009.

5

'The best thing that ever happened to me'

ON A QUIET summer day in 1996, by when she had been in Ward 12 for eight months, Mum said to me, *'I'm looking forward to seeing Dad again... I didn't have long enough with Dad, only twenty-eight years.'*

During the thirty-two months that she spent in hospital her thoughts often turned to him, memories happy and sad.

Once she told me, *'I thanked Dad for a lot of things a couple of days ago, more than ever before... He was a lovely husband and father... We had lovely times with Dad...*

'He was too good for me, but he always thought that I was better than I was. Florrie shouldn't have made so much of me to Charlie* and he shouldn't have told Dad that I'd been so good taking care of my parents: that's where the mistake was made...

'I'd love to hear Dad laugh now, to see him laugh... I loved his dry Cornish jokes... How much he loved you boys... Oxford University

---

* Florrie was Dad's sister; Charlie, her husband. They were 'matchmakers' for Mum and Dad.

was his plan for you both... He was generous and gentle, always on the side of the loser, the one in need...

'*He was the best thing that ever happened to me...*

'*Will you always think about Dad? I hope that he gets the reward that he deserves for being so lovely. He already has it, I think... Lovely Dad... God bless Dad from all of us. Thank you, Dad, for everything, for being so lovely to us. Thanks be to Dad, thanks be to God.*

'*Going on walks on those happy days with Dad, and Rusty, and sitting on the grass bank among the celandines by the hedge and eating cheese sandwiches together in February... We went picking up chestnuts every year at Windwhistle Wood. Dad loved doing that.*

'*We had lovely outings with Dad... He was a very peaceful man... When I worried about having size eight shoes, he said,* "Don't worry, Grace, big stones are needed for the foundation of a church, and, with your 5'10", you need size eight." *The dear of him; I cheered up... I'm glad I had Jack for my husband... He was very clever to do what he did in life... Take care of his MBE, won't you? ...*

'*Dad was lovely, wasn't he...?*

'*I was almost* too *happy with him...*'

A month before Mum died, on the last visit when she could speak to me, I showed her a photo of Dad. I did that on so many visits. She recognised him immediately and her face came alive, '*I love that photo.*'

And looking at the photo, she said to Dad, '*God bless you, my darling.*'

PART TWO

6

'... down to Oxford's towers'

EARLY IN THE EVENING of a day in late July 1972, I parked a blue MG Midget sports car carefully at the side of the quiet road that runs along the ridge of Boar's Hill. It was not many days after Dad's funeral. There was no other car in sight. Mum and I struggled out of the low leather seats. We crossed the road and leant on a five-bar gate.

We gazed down at Oxford far beyond the fields in which black and white Friesian cattle grazed. The air was clear. With Dad's binoculars, brought back from India, we could pick out the towers and spires of churches and colleges, even the graceful curves of the Sheldonian Theatre and the Radcliffe Camera, golden in the sunset.

Mum soaked in the view. It was the first time that she had glimpsed what, at such cost to them, she and Dad had enabled my brother and me to enjoy.

Dad never saw that view.

Mum and I drove down into Oxford, over the River Isis and up St Aldate's. The streets were empty. It was as if the High and the Broad, Magdalen Bridge and St Giles, the whole of Oxford, had reserved these few minutes for Mum alone, to take in all its beauty and grace, chaste and pure of every other person and impression.

Knowing that this experience would never be repeated, I drove back to Boar's Hill. Again, we stood at the gate and fed on what we saw in the distance.

'*I can't go on,*' Mum said. She was suddenly weighed down by the harsh contrast between the glory before us and the loss of Dad after their twenty-eight years together. Many of those years had been dominated by Huntington's, the hereditary disease from which Dad had suffered for so long and which slowly, so slowly, killed him; the children of a sufferer stand a fifty-fifty chance of developing it.

'You've got to go on,' I said. 'If you give up, we're finished.'

Mum knew that it was true. She formed an iron will and never yielded.

We turned away from Boar's Hill and Oxford. We made our way to Ely. Judy had already returned there after Dad's funeral, and she was waiting to welcome Mum on her first visit to stay with us for a few days.

Mum and I never again spoke to each other of our conversation on Boar's Hill. We never told anyone else of it. She treasured Dad in her heart, and between the two of them, she and Dad, and the resolution that she formed on Boar's Hill, saved us all.

7
A New Life

AFTER HER RETURN to Number 10 from Ely, Mum began to build a new life. It took time.

For years taking care of Dad had been the centre of everything. And, for all the problems and sadness, they had still found happiness together. Running Number 10, walks with Rusty, their Labrador, lunch in the kitchen by the Rayburn, another walk and afternoon tea by the fire in the sitting-room, telephone calls in the evening to Wally, and visits from Hilda and Fred – all this had seen them through the last years of Dad's illness. The exercise and good meals kept them fit. Every morning they went into the country, usually a walk of two or three miles to Chaddlewood or Newnham, followed by their 'peasant food' stew of meat and vegetables and potatoes, all cooked in one pot on the Rayburn, by whose gentle warmth they sat as they ate it.

Dad had spent the last three years of his life at Moorhaven Hospital. Mum visited him three times a week, by bus. During the last four or five months she went there every day, a round trip of twenty or more miles. *'The staff are so kind and gentle. Did I tell you that one young male nurse said that Dad was "a contented bloke"?'* She was thrilled when he immediately spelt 'trigonometry' for her when she needed that word in a crossword. *'It was a good visit today,'* she wrote to me, *'Dad said, "We've had* some happy times together" *when I reminded him about our walks with Rusty.'*

When Dad died in 1972, it was on the feast day of St Mary Magdalen. It gave us comfort that Dad had passed from us on the day of the disciple who had been the first to see the Risen Christ, at daybreak on Easter Day.

Ten years after Dad's death, I found two colour photographs of him and Mum taken in the Devon countryside. I sent them to Mum on the anniversary of his death. *'A joyful experience at 7.30 this morning… I am delighted with the snaps. I love the one of Dad and me in the gate. It made me feel so strange. We were so happy. It was very exciting for me.'*

Mum's new life would last twenty-three years at home and then nearly three in hospital.

There were two setbacks in the first couple of years. Hilda died of pneumonia in January 1973, leaving Fred a widower. At the end of October 1974, Rusty died.

Each of them left a big gap.

Nearly twenty years later, Mum attended the eightieth birthday party of an old friend. Nicknamed Gussie, the friend had lived across the road from Mum's family at Stone Barton in the 1930s. She had been struck by Mum's character and integrity when she was a young woman in her twenties. 'There was something special about her even then,' she told me after Mum's death.

A group of widows at Gussie's party were sitting together, enjoying their lunch. Mum was listening to their conversation. 'I don't know who I miss more – my husband or my dog,' one of them commented. That doubt did not arise in Mum's case, but she grieved for Rusty, too. She missed their walks and the memories of countless similar walks with Dad.

Step by step Mum created a new routine that gave her life shape and purpose.

Each day began early. Before she got dressed, she prayed at her bedside. Then she opened the front door to bring in the milk-bottle from the doorstep and greeted the light with the words, '*The Glory of the Lord*', and '*I will lift up mine eyes unto the hills from whence cometh my help, even from the Lord*' as she looked over the village towards Dorsmouth Rock, the hill between Plympton and Saltram.

Mum had a good breakfast beside the Rayburn. By the end of her time at Number 10, it took her hours to get up and prepare it. She would find herself sitting at the breakfast table, gazing out of the window at the forsythia in March; the blue-tits feeding their young in the nesting box in April and May; the 'Star of India' clematis in June; and (after the death of Mr Pearse, her neighbour at Number 8) a dark-green bay-tree towering up from beyond the garden-wall. '*What would Mr Pearse have thought of that?*' she asked – and she knew the answer. Mr Pearse used to keep his garden so neat that he would cut wandering blades of grass with a pair of nail scissors, and root out weeds with a special trowel attached to a long wooden handle, which he devised when he grew too stiff to bend down to attack them.

After breakfast she read her Bible. It is heavily worn. Her favourite passage in the New Testament – the page is thread-bare and stained from her constant reference to it – was from the first letter of St Peter, chapter one:

'Blessed be the God and Father of our Lord Jesus Christ. Through His great mercy we are born again to a living hope through the resurrection of Christ Jesus from the dead.'

On a piece of paper, now dog-eared and much repaired, among the prayers that she used every day, she had written these words:

'O Lord, the God of all strength,
We pray that you will comfort and help all who are in
*   trouble, sickness or distress.*
Reveal yourself to them that they may know your peace,
Through Jesus Christ, Our Lord. Amen.'

Between the pages of her Bible is a text which she cut from the personal column of the newspaper one day and on which she used to meditate: *'I wish above all things that thou mayest prosper and be in health, even as thy soul prospereth'* (3 John, verse 2).

Mum prayed unceasingly that we might be spared Huntington's chorea. Her sense of responsibility for the risk we faced and her grief were overwhelming, but she knew that to express them to us, except very occasionally, would be dangerous. In her diary, at one difficult period, she wrote: *'I am sorry to have brought such sadness to my family.'* In fact, she and Dad were utterly innocent: they could not have understood the situation in the 1940s.

She would have preferred to be at risk herself, rather than the two of us. She wished that this were possible with force and sincerity, as great a sacrifice as one person can offer for another, as if she gave up her own life repeatedly for us, day by day.

Alongside her faith, Mum's stubbornness and simplicity sustained her. She could be shrewd and wise, take a long view of disasters and see them turning into successes, endure all manner of sorrows and yet take joy in life. She could always tap into the deepest wells of her heart, the heart of the child who had made darts from pins, corks and chicken feathers; who had identified with 'Jakey', the patient donkey, pulling the trap with the children to a Sunday school outing at the beach at Wembury; who had made marmalade from orange peel in a tin can over a fire in the back-garden.

Mum delighted in things that cost little or nothing. In hospital one day, very near the end of her life, she opened her eyes as I arrived on a visit and said, *'I've been thinking about apple blossom.'*

Almost as soon as Mum had washed up the dishes, Fred used to call on her for coffee and cheese and biscuits. On his way to or from work at the police station my cousin Jack often dropped in to see that all was well and stayed for a while.

After the Second World War, Fred had settled down as a driver for the Electricity Board. He had become utterly reliable and steady, a man of good humour and gentle kindness.

In their many years as widower and widow, Fred and Mum were the best of friends. She used to remind him occasionally that at his wedding the vicar had enjoined him to take good care of Hilda with the words, 'Do not let this beautiful flower fade.' The Vicar had noticed, with some alarm, that Fred had arrived for the service wearing two left boots.

Fred took all the old stories from Mum in good part. The horror of all that he had seen in the Army when he was present at the opening of the concentration camp at Belsen sometimes took its toll on his nerves, but after a few days in hospital he again became stoical, generous, mild and full of sympathetic humour, a very present help in trouble to Mum and others. They were faithful friends.

Fred was as fond of the elevenses with Mum as she was pleased to see him. If the weather was kind, they would go into the garden to see what was growing. They used to count the flowers on the clematis and the roses.

The gardens, front and back, grew more and more important to Mum as each of the twenty-three years after Dad's death passed. The back garden was overgrown but beautiful and peaceful. When we had arrived in 1950 there had been a lilac tree and a New Dawn rose. As the 1970s and 1980s passed, a mass of flowering, fragrant shrubs and clematis grew up there. An apple tree, grown from a core in the 1950s, stood fifteen feet tall; it produced its first fruit a few weeks before the stroke that took Mum away from home forever. A bitter cherry tree rose up to twenty or more feet, and had to be pruned when it reached the electricity wires supplying the terrace. Weigelia, deutzia, daphne mezereum, ferns from Dartmoor, a holly tree, and a fig tree were all packed into the sun-trap of this small walled garden.

In the garden at the front of the house Mum and Dad had inherited or planted viburnum fragrans, daphne odora and daphne mezereum, a miniature Japanese lilac, chaenomales (japonica), white azalea which, every May, produced an expanse of white flowers (*'like an angel's wings,'* Mum said), a viburnum bodnantense with an intoxicating scent, forsythia, a carpet of bluebells, wallflowers, and kaffir lilies (schistostyles). Beside the front gate there was a tiny rose bush which had been there since Victorian times, perhaps put there by Number 10's first owners. This rose produced a flower, its first for some years, and then died, in the year of Mum's death.

After an hour or so with Mum, Fred went for a pint of beer and something to eat with his friends at the Constitutional Club in Ridgeway.

Occasionally Fred took Mum and Gussie for a drive. *'Fred and Gussie took me to Burrator reservoir. We walked right around the lake, arriving home at 6.45. We saw the most wonderful scenery imaginable and on arriving at Sheepstor village we almost knocked down a heron resting by a stream, the nearest I have ever been. We saw a buzzard, two sparrow hawks, jays galore, long-tailed tits, marsh tits, mallard, pintail ducks, gulls, shags, magpies, and robins. It was a perfect bird-watching afternoon. The trees were all colours and the bells of Sheepstor village church rang merrily all the way around in practice for today's service. What a magic time, four hours at Burrator! I treated them to thick Williams's ice cream wafers the thickest clotted cream ever... Fred strolled along, leaning on his walking stick, like a belted earl. Hilda would have been tickled pink to see him.'*

On most days Mum cooked her 'peasant food' for lunch. She listened to the 'Afternoon Theatre' play on Radio 4 at the kitchen table. As her hearing worsened and listening to the radio became more difficult, she began to watch films on the television in the afternoon. She made a fire in the sitting-room and ate her tea (her favourite meal) beside it, in her armchair, part of the three-piece suite which her brother Arthur had given their parents. Dad had had it re-upholstered in the early 1960s. Once when she was telling me about all the films that she had enjoyed by the fire, she said, *'One does not get old without getting artful.'*

Mum built her life on routine; she contemplated life, and the world, and the beyond. This made life possible for her. *'Having a fire; doing some weeding when you feel like it; doing the crossword by the fire – it all helps,'* she said to me.

Sometimes she found it difficult to get going with her housework. *'I've been reading St. Paul's letters to the Thessalonians and this morning's piece says,* "If anyone will not work, let him not eat." *So I think I'd better get on with some work.'*

The evenings were tedious in winter, but in summer Mum enjoyed the sunsets through her sitting-room window – golden, opal, aquamarine. As the evening star began to shine, she put out her empty milk bottle, brightly polished, on the front doorstep for the milkman to collect the next morning. She looked across Moorland Road to Number 3, near the turning into Ridgeway, to check that the light was shining in Mrs Wyndham Hull's bedroom, showing that she was safe. Every night Mrs Wyndham Hull did the same for Mum.

Peggy, my mother-in-law, did a lot to help Mum.

She had lost her husband, Noel, eighteen months before Dad died. The two of them often spoke on the telephone, with Peggy reporting to Mum on some of the trips she made to stay with us. Mum loved to hear this news. She was touched by the way that Peggy helped her face the loss of Dad. She often spoke to me about this.

In the early spring of 1973, soon after Hilda's death, Peggy p 43 first drove over from her home near Ottery St Mary in East Devon to visit Mum. She stayed a night.

For Peggy's arrival Mum had brought down from the top shelf of the kitchen cupboard a coffee-pot that she hardly ever used. She forgot to warm it on the Rayburn. Until her dying day she regretted that she gave Peggy lukewarm coffee that morning.

The two of them found it easy to talk. They had in common their time in India. After Sandhurst, Peggy's husband had served many years in the Indian Army. Their family back-grounds had been totally different, and this made Mum feel all the more fortunate that they got on so well and it added to the interest of their talks.

Mum had already taken Judy to her heart. In a letter to her at this time she wrote, *'Did I ever tell you that you are a comfort to me, Judy?'*

She never met Noel but she had heard of his kindness as Vicar of Wembury. *'There is a lady I ride with on the bus to Moorhaven who comes from Wembury. She told me that Judy's father was a wonderful clergyman and went to see everyone, no matter whether they were church or chapel or didn't go anywhere at all. She was sad to hear that he had died.'*

Peggy's visit went well.

'I took Peggy her early morning tea in bed when she stayed with me and her pretty face came up from under the bedclothes...

'We went for a walk through the pathfields to St Maurice and sat on the top of the castle mound for a long time in the sunshine, looking at the view over Plympton, the cottages and the lawn at the bottom where children were playing...

'Peggy enjoyed the roast beef that I cooked for her...

'It is easy to like Peggy.'

After the visit Peggy wrote to me. *'I thoroughly enjoyed being with your mother and she was very good to me. She sat on my bed while we drank our early morning tea...I'm so glad that she is going away to Scotland with your brother. It will give her lots to think about for a long time afterwards... The house was beautifully warm! I've just had a visit from the Samaritan leader from Exeter and I hope to join them if I'm approved.'*

Mum did go to Scotland, for a tour of the Highlands at Easter. It was the only time that she left Rusty in kennels. She had always wanted to see Scotland because of her father's enthusiastic stories about his visits there.

Peggy's forecast was proved right. *'I had a wonderful holiday in Scotland. I shall never forget it...'*

Peggy stayed with Mum a second time eighteen months

later. *'I had a little chat with Peggy on the phone yesterday. I rang to congratulate her on her son's wedding and to wish them all health and happiness ... On Thursday Peggy is coming for a day and night, so I had better put the milk on the Rayburn for coffee!'*

Peggy took Mum a jar of apple pickle, some dessert apples and a bunch of pinks from her wonderful garden at West Hill in the country between Ottery St Mary and Sidmouth. They had become firm friends and sat by the fire and talked. *'I was sorry when she went. How well she looks,'* Mum wrote.

At the time of Peggy's visit Miss Walker, the vet, told Mum that Rusty's days were numbered, and a week later he died of cancer.

Only a month before that Rusty had enjoyed his last walk to Newnham House, the home of the Cobbold family. Mr Cobbold had married a daughter of the Strodes, the family to which the house had belonged for many years. He had often talked to Dad and Mum on their walks with Rusty in the 1960s when he was out and about working on the estate. He had encouraged them to use the long abandoned, hidden lower drive from Newnham House on their way back to Plympton. This spared them the constant danger from the heavily-loaded lorries which pounded their way down the road from the china clay pits at Lee Moor.

As Mum was looking over the gate at the Georgian house where her father had been butler sixty years earlier, *'A car drew up and it was Mr Cobbold. He was very concerned that he hadn't seen me for months. I told him that Rusty is now ten years old and not as energetic as he was. We had a long talk ... He invited me to come to the house and see them. I would love to visit them and see it. I have never been in the house although I used to walk there with my father. It is good to have such a nice friend to meet on my walks.'*

Mum thought a lot about Newnham House. *'Newnham House intrigues me. I gaze at it and think of my father slaving there as a butler for twenty-three shillings a week to keep eight children and then I think of the salaries people have today and great family allowances. It just proves that money doesn't bring happiness as my parents were a model of marital bliss. Anyhow, I feel a bit of a communist when I think how people slaved for a piteous reward.'*

In January 1975 my brother was married. Mum was happy. She wrote of his bride: *'She is kind, thoughtful, tolerant and good company. It was a most awful muddle here when they came on my birthday and she said that it made her feel at home.'*

When the engagement was announced, Mum wrote, *'I am very happy about this marriage. She is a dear. They are well suited. Dad would have loved his two daughters-in-law. I have just been looking at his picture and thinking how happy he would have been with his sons married to two such lovely girls.'*

We drove across Devon through deserted lanes to the wedding. Uncle Fred came with us in our Morris Minor. We stopped for a break and watched the birds at a little bridge over a stream in the depths of the North Devon countryside. We almost made ourselves late.

'It was a lovely wedding,' wrote Mum.

In May 1975 we took Mum to visit Peggy. It would be the last time they saw each other. *'I so much enjoyed going to Ottery St Mary and seeing Peggy's new house… I thought that she was looking well and it will be lovely when she is better. It was a day to remember.'*

In June I had to give Mum the bad news that Peggy's cancer had spread – a possibility that she had probably mentioned to Mum on her last visit to Number 10. Later Mum wrote to me, *'I'm feeling very sad about Peggy. Will you and Judy tell me if there is* anything *I can do? I am very fond of her – she has a lovely nature. Your news is such a shock that my brain is not functioning properly. I have shed a lot of tears this morning.'*

At the end of August Peggy died. She was the same age as Mum.

Mum was devastated by her death. In her diary, on the day before the funeral, she wrote, *'Today I feel lonely.'* The following day she read the full burial service from the Prayer Book at home as the service was being conducted.

'If only she could have had five more years... I'm very glad that I knew her – a lovely person. Each time I go into the entrance to St Maurice pathfields I think of our walk together. It was just after the new road was made and I could not find the entrance. Peggy said, "Is this the way?" We were both amused that she found it although I have lived here so long.'

At St Mary's church on the Sunday after the funeral Mum became upset about Peggy's death. She told me that she *'had to come out of church'*, midway through the Holy Communion service.

Happy memories of Peggy stayed strong with Mum. Year by year she remembered Peggy's birthday on the sixth of June. *'I thought yesterday of a lovely person whose birthday it would have been.'* Later, in hospital she often spoke of Peggy's kindness to her and of her affection for her. She reminded me of a visit she had paid to her in her cottage at West Hill. *'I remember the flowers and butterflies at her cottage. She gave me some lovely soup, and when I told her that I liked it she said it was "only out of a tin"... She used to say that if she didn't make a pudding, she'd be happy with bread and marmalade. Sometimes she used to eat it before going to bed.*

'She was a lovely person, and I got on very well with her. I liked her a lot...'

Mum was tempted to have a new dog. Her brother Jack offered her *'a Labrador puppy for my birthday, but I refused as there can be only one dog for me.'*

She did not often see Jack, but he used to send her an occasional rabbit or pigeon until his death in 1976. There were many local countrymen at his funeral at St Mary's church, the final generation of a type of Englishman who had, for centuries, lived that sort of rustic life. Mr Matthews, the Vicar, who also enjoyed pigeon or rabbit stew, said in his address that Jack was *'one of the old school who lived close to nature'*. Jack had never been registered with a doctor under the National Health Service until the stroke that killed him after three days in hospital.

Soon after that Mum lay awake all night because she had seen a litter of Labrador puppies. *'They are entrancing, but I must be strong and decline. Sadly, I am getting on in years.'*

A few weeks after Peggy's passing Mrs Rothwell, another good friend, died. Mrs Rothwell had grown up at Penzance in west Cornwall. She had moved to Plympton with her husband in the 1930s, and she and Dad had often talked about Cornwall. She was one of those who could see beyond the effects of Huntington's to the real Dad, and did not let the illness affect her attitude towards him. Her kind, matter-of-fact attitude meant a lot to Mum, who attended her funeral in early November. *'It is very sad. I wish that I had gone to see her more often.'*

It was the beginning of a long, hard winter.

8

Windwhistle

IN THE 1970s British Rail introduced a new fleet of high-speed trains on the Western Region line from Paddington station to Penzance. These trains made the journey to Plymouth in a little less than three hours at their best, and comfortably in three and a half hours.

There was a wonderful timetable. From time to time I could visit Mum for the day on a Saturday.

At Paddington I went to the front of the train and settled down in a seat next door to the guard's compartment, with my back to the engine. At times the train accelerated suddenly to top speed. Sometimes the driver had to brake sharply, and the pungent, acrid smell of the brakes lingered in the air for a while.

Few people used the 7.25 train in the winter months. It can never have paid its way. In those strange years that seemed not to matter. I sometimes felt that the train had been laid on especially for me. I strode from one end of it to the other to buy tea or coffee or simply for the exercise as I recovered from my week's work bent over a desk.

In Plymouth I took a taxi and reached Number 10 by 11 o'clock. Often Uncle Fred was there, '*ever faithful*' in Mum's words, and she gave us coffee by the Rayburn. Uncle Fred went on his way, and Mum cooked us pasties or roast beef. After that we went for a walk, and then had tea by the fire in the sitting-room. Then I would be off by taxi to catch the 6.35 train, getting home before 11pm.

On one Saturday in early February the sun was unusually warm. Mum and I packed two of her pasties (golden brown and just out of the oven) in a blue tea-cosy decorated with various garden birds. We set off on a long walk. We visited the lanes through which Mum and Dad had walked with us and the old push-chair in the early 1950s.

We walked past the Plantation and up Stuggy Lane, alongside the railway line. We went under the railway bridge, and up the hill, past the *'chimney pot'*, a pottery chute through which the winter rainwater from the drains under the fields gushed on its way to cascade down the hill. As a little boy I had stood and gazed at this mysterious sight and fished with a hazel stick in the torrential stream.

Mum and I pressed on to West Park Hill. We walked on the footpath through the fields to the village of Hemerdon. Beyond the village we made a seat among the bright yellow celandines on the bank of a high hedge. In the distance we could see the waters of Plymouth Sound and the cliffs of Cornwall.

We set about the pasties, still hot and steaming.

Judy asked Mum for advice about making pasties. *'Plain flour, for me, is essential. Self-raising flour soaks up the juice into it. My idea is that onion is very important and I use a medium one in each for juice, and a bit of turnip* [swede is called turnip in Devon and Cornwall] *cut small and of course, potato. Just lately I've used skirt. I would never have done so in the past – I always used best steak. So after rolling the pastry and placing the meat, potato, turnip and onion on it, I put a knob of butter or marge on top before closing it all in. No, I don't soak the vegetables, Judy. I bet your pasties turn out lovely!'*

After an hour there taking in the view from Hemerdon and watching the birds and some horses in a field, we stirred ourselves. We walked back through Windwhistle Wood and down the lower drive from Newnham House, overgrown with gigantic rhododendrons. After we had had a cup of tea and a slice of her Madeira cake, Mum played Elgar's 'Chanson de

Matin' and 'To Music' by Schubert. The taxi arrived to take me to the railway station. '*I shall not forget today,*' Mum wrote; nor would I.

Occasionally I stayed the Saturday night at Number 10. Normally we went to Holy Communion at eight o'clock at St Mary's, but one Sunday we woke up very early and went for a walk instead. There was something about the clear air, the sharp frost, and the sense of the passing years and the changes coming to Plympton that said 'Go now. You may never have this chance again.'

We walked out to the Tory Brook, where a bridge crossed the stream on the way to Torridge. Mum had played there as a child, wriggling her toes in the mud in the summers before the First World War. That morning the edges of the stream were frozen.

We walked on to the Plantation, meeting one of the regular couples setting out for the eight o'clock service. Apart from them, all was still and silent. We stood and watched a pair of bullfinches playing in the hedge, their breasts seeming redder and their rumps whiter than ever in the clear air and bright sunshine. This quiet scene held us in a trance.

As we reached the crest of the hill, we met Mrs Gratton, standing at the gate of her house, 'Twin Oaks'. Mum's brother, Jack, had worked for her and Colonel Gratton for many years. Jack and Colonel Gratton had both been great country-men, walking the woods together, each with his shotgun, accompanied by Jack's dogs. When he could no longer do the gardening for her, Mrs Gratton continued to send Uncle Jack a bottle of whisky and a Stilton cheese at Christmas.

At the Plantation we looked up and down the railway line, hoping for a train. Mum recalled how often she and her family had stood there, waving to relatives setting off on some journey. '*We were great wavers,*' she said.

We walked back to Number 10 for porridge and a boiled egg. Then I was away to London.

9

Neighbours and Friends

ON MIDSUMMER'S DAY one year Mum wrote to me:

'The weather is superb. I go out early to the shops and then spend the day mooching in the house and watering and admiring the garden. I've been saving water for months; we've had weeks of dry, sunny weather. The "Star of India" clematis has the most lovely dark, velvety flowers with a red stripe. The "blue" rose in the back garden is terrific, one mass of parma violet colour, and the hebe is about to flower. The Penelope rose, in the front garden, is falling now after a fantastic show ...

'I have just been sitting on Mr Pearse's garden seat with him in his front garden for twenty minutes. I left before he told me to go: quite a shock for him!

'Saw a marvellous film yesterday afternoon...Shall soon be preparing my peasant food: one onion, a small slice of braising steak, one potato, with lots of cabbage ... Then I proceed to the sitting-room to see my film, do two lines of the rug, read dear old Woman's Weekly, *have tea, water the garden, television, bed ...'*

Sometimes the day did not start so well:

'This morning I got up feeling very grumpy and tired from all the work I have been doing for Mr Short while Kathleen has been in hospital. The weather is abominable, too.

'I was sitting on the arm of the chair in the sitting-room when a red bus went by in Moorland Road. Written on it in big letters were the words "It's a wonderful world". Very funny, and that brought me to my senses.'

Although she saw quite a lot of her immediate neighbours (the Pearses and the Shorts), Mum practised solitude and simplicity. In hospital, dreaming of a return to Number 10, which she knew could never take place, she said: *'I want to be plain and ordinary. If you can just be* nothing, *and get along every day like that, it's much better than being something. Just being* quiet: *that's lovely, isn't it?'*

It was true, but there was more to it. Mum did love quiet and solitude, but she also sometimes relished company. All the old Plymptonians knew her, and so did many of the newcomers. She was popular. Something about her stayed in the mind and affection of those whom she had known or worked with decades earlier.

It was as if she filled a spot in people's hearts or souls that would otherwise have been empty. On one of her rare visits to buy clothes in Plymouth when she was well into her sixties, she called in at Spooner's department store. In the hosiery department Mum approached a counter where the assistant was bent almost double, peering into the bottom drawer of the cabinet and unable to see who was approaching.

'Can you help me with…?' Mum began.

'Of course I can, Grace,' replied the assistant, without looking up from the drawer. It was a one-time colleague of Mum's at Yeo's. They had not seen each other for almost fifty years.

Mum could not understand why people had changed and become so discontented as they became richer after the Second World War. The endless strikes and turmoil in the 1970s troubled her. *'The railway strikes are abating, but the situation in the hospitals is tragic. The world is certainly more discontented since the War… What hope is there if all people want is wage increases?*

*Patriotism is almost dead…It will be lovely when the country returns
to its senses… In church on Sunday evening we had a talk from a
visiting missionary from Africa. Listening to him, I realised that it is
here that we need to spread the Word.'*

Time was beginning to race.

One afternoon Mr Pearse gave Mum a lift to St Mary's
church for the funeral of their old friend and neighbour,
Mr Bailey. Afterwards, standing and talking at the front garden
fence between Number 8 and Number 10, Mr Pearse said to
Mum, *'They're taking them from our pen now.'*

It was natural for Walter Pearse to refer in that way to a
'pen' of cattle or pigs at Plympton market when speaking of the
increasing trickle of funerals at St Mary's of members of his,
and in due course Mum's, generation. Like his father before
him, Mr Pearse and his brother Frank had run the family firm
of Auctioneers and Estate Agents. He had a booming voice,
recognised far and wide when he was acting as auctioneer. He
was a Fellow of the Royal Institution of Chartered Surveyors
and the Chartered Auctioneers and Estate Agents. He loved the
land and the farming way of life that was still so important in
the village. Until the end of the 1950s Plympton and Plymptonians smelt comfortably, reassuringly of farming.*

At Plympton Market over the years 'Mr Walter', one of three
brothers, had specialised in pigs and his brother, 'Mr Frank',
in cattle. Walter stood up for his animals: 'Even a pig grunts,'
he would say to Mum when she thanked him for some kind
action towards her.

Even as some of her age-group began to die, Mum remained
something of a village character. *'I love Plympton,'* she said to

---

* Plympton Market survived, on a small scale, until it was destroyed by the
foot-and-mouth disaster on beef farms in 2001.

me in hospital, *'even the word – the "p" in the middle –* **Plymp-pton***.'* And she uttered the word quietly but explosively.

She would sometimes spend a full morning in Ridgeway, buying a few groceries at Mr Kelly's shop and visiting Muldowney's, the newsagent. She spent most of the time talking to old friends, who seemed somehow to queue up to talk to her. Sometimes she might not have seen one of them for years. Once she said to a man twenty years younger than herself: *'You* do *remind me of my brother Harry.'* 'It's not surprising, Auntie Grace,' he replied. 'I'm Harry's son, your nephew Cyril!' This happened not once but on two occasions, separated by several years. She told this story against herself many times.

Mum professed not to enjoy social gatherings, but sometimes she was energised and animated by them. She begrudged herself any special clothes for these rare events. She attended a supper party organised for the Christian Stewardship campaign at St Mary's, happily dressed in her favourite mustard-coloured jumper and brown pinafore dress. She was so excited by being with so many people that she was unable to get to sleep that night.

But it was meeting the 'eight-o'clockers', the regular worshippers at the early Holy Communion service at St Mary's, that gave Mum her main social gathering each week. Sunday by Sunday her diary records:

'8 o'clock Communion,' and *'6.30 Evensong.'*

It is sad to read week by week, in her last years at home, *'No Holy Communion,'* as she began to suffer more often from varicose ulcers on her legs. She struggled hard to get there into her eighties.

In the service the Confession and Absolution stirred her deeply. In her own word, the prayers made her 'snort' sometimes. Mum's view of her sins was completely out of line with the truth, but she also had, as if in compensation, an overwhelming sense of God's glory and mercy. Unconsciously she joined in with the priest's words, *'Therefore with angels and archangels and all the company of Heaven we laud and magnify Thy glorious name, evermore praising Thee and saying...',* before the congregation joins in with the acclamation, *'... Holy, Holy, Holy, Lord God of Hosts...'*

After the service Mum often walked back to 'Skew Bridge' over the railway line with her old friend Dorothy, before turning around and heading home for breakfast.

Dorothy and her husband 'Bim' had known Mum and Dad from their first days in Plympton, in 1959. Not knowing that they were taking the pew usually occupied by Mum and Dad, they had begun to sit at Evensong in the back pew in the north aisle. For a few weeks Mum and Dad slipped into the pew ahead of them. 'Bim' gradually noticed Dad's choreic movements caused by Huntington's. He sensed that it was embarrassing for Mum and Dad to have others sitting behind them. They moved forward a row and Mum and Dad went back to their old pew. Mum's great affection for Dorothy and 'Bim' went back to that kind act.

Mum must often have been lonely, despite the comfort of the routine that she built. She rarely told us about it. She never asked anything of us. She knew that we came to visit her as often as we could. She believed that often a trouble shared is a trouble passed to another. In her diaries, for all their brief entries, there are hints of days when her solitude became loneliness.

Years later she would tell me something that related to it as a joke. Sometimes, after we had left Number 10 to go back to London, Mum sat at the kitchen table and *'howled'*. Through the party wall Mrs Short heard Mum wailing. She went in to see her for a cup of tea, taking with her, perhaps, a slice of the wonderful Victoria sponge that she used to bake, spread through with blackberry jam made from the brambles growing on her back garden wall. Kathleen had suffered from diabetes since her youth and could not eat the cakes that she made for Gordon, her cantankerous, truculent but well-meaning husband.

Once, the sadness of Dad's illness and death, and her sense of loss at the end of our visit, overwhelmed Mum. She wailed to Mrs Short, *'Kathleen, I wasn't good enough for Jack.'*

Of all the people whom I had known as a child, Kathleen, I suppose, had the shrewdest, most detached eye for character and behaviour. She had liked Dad and respected him, and she continued to speak openly of him as a real person, after his illness and death. That was rare. An illness like Huntington's tends to freeze the onlooker's normal humanity and stop him behaving normally. It is easy to understand, but Mrs Short's open attitude was balm to the soul. So, understanding Mum through and through, she replied, 'Of course you weren't good enough for him, Grace. We all know *that*.' With these words Kathleen rescued Mum from despair.

To the end of her life the words, 'Of course you weren't, Grace,' gave Mum comfort. They always triggered her laughter.

Gordon had worked as a tailor and as a commercial traveller in his time, taking goods to the small farms of south Devon. He was an awkward customer. *'Poor Kathleen,'* Mum used to say.

Sometimes Gordon would meet someone coming to visit Mum on the doorstep. *'Go in there and you'll find Grace sitting down,'* Mr Short used to say to them, much to Mum's disgust. He could not come to terms with Mum's quietist nature. He was driven by a nervous anxiety and tension that seemed ill-matched to the stately game of bowls that he and Mr Pearse used to play on summer afternoons. Plympton was blessed with an unexpectedly beautiful cricket ground and bowling green. But it was her contemplative attitude that enabled Mum to cope with what she had to endure, to relish all the joys she found, and contentedly to live a life that others would have found lonely.

Gordon was always ready to pick a quarrel. He attended public meetings and raised difficult issues in order to provoke those who disagreed with him. Soon after one meeting and a fierce public row with Gordon, an elderly man suffered a heart attack.

At one time he and Kathleen considered having a lodger to balance their budget. *'The lodger would need nerves of iron,'* Mum said, but Mrs Short received a legacy from a relative and the need for money from a lodger went away.

Gordon was sometimes so rude to her that Mum wrote, *'I almost hate him. A very religious lady said to Fred, "He's a bugger." Sorry about the language, but I thought it would make you laugh. I was surprised as she is a regular churchgoer and very proper. It just shows that even really good people can be driven over the edge ... Gordon offered to let me take away a lot of rotten wood for the fire from his appalling garden gate, but I'm not quite such a fool as I look.'*

One afternoon when Gordon took Kathleen out for a drive, he spoilt the effect by saying loudly, 'I bloody well don't care where we go!' And on another occasion he called out to a friend as he and Kathleen set off to a funeral, 'We never go out so we might as well go to a funeral.' *'Kathleen just laughed,'* Mum told me.

'An awful man,' Mum said, yet she found it impossible truly to dislike him: *'At bottom we're good neighbours. What do you think? Mr Short told me that I radiated kindness. Wasn't that nice of him?'*

Gordon himself had a strong streak of kindness. He was easily moved to sympathy and genuine tears by the suffering of others. Both he and Kathleen were sincere Methodists. Their only child had died of measles when very young. They were anxious when we caught it at school, and urged Mum and Dad to keep the curtains drawn to protect our eyesight. The loss of their little boy continued to affect them deeply.

Gordon had a quixotic loyalty and sense of honour. He remained an Asquithian Liberal during the deepest days of that party's decline. Kathleen kept her own counsel on politics, as she did on so much else.

Occasionally Gordon gave Mum a lift into Plymouth in his Jowett Javelin motor-car, even at that date a collector's item, of which he was rightly proud. He sold it for a good price and bought a Morris Minor, which he called a 'Morris Eight', thinking of the 1930s version. Sitting on seats whose springs had long lost their resilience, he and Mum used to sing music-hall songs and Wesley's hymns as Gordon drove erratically into town. He told Mum how much he liked the granite headstone that we had chosen with such care for Dad's grave. *'He was down at Plympton cattle market and took a look at Dad's stone. He really admired it and could see that it was really done especially for Dad.'*

In later years Gordon slept for a while in the afternoon on a sofa in their front sitting-room. When she went in to visit Kathleen, Mum would catch sight of Gordon's upper dentures, carefully placed on the back of the sofa.

Gordon owned a pianola. For years he delighted in pretending to Mum and everyone else that he was an accomplished pianist. One lady commented to Mum, 'I can forgive Mr Short anything for being such a musician.'

Gordon saw the joke. He knew his faults, and that was endearing.

Mum's neighbours at Number 8, Walter and Nancy Pearse, became a source of comfort and helped her face her new life. The three of them became good friends.

Soon after we arrived in 1950 Walter put up a fence between his front garden and ours; the two had previously merged the one into the other. He wanted to protect himself from two young noisy boys and their raucous friends. He complained that we already had the lungs and volume of voice to equip us for his job at Plympton market. He planted shrubs along the fence. Over the years things were gradually transformed. What began life as a barrier became a source of shared delight, laden with azalea, viburnum and japonica.

Walter and his brothers had been brought up by their father in a hard school. Their forebears had been farmers in South

Devon for three hundred years. Walter's father, in particular, had built up a successful business. He gave his three sons a strict upbringing, teaching them discipline, honesty and the value of money.

The family had lived in a lovely old house, Barncott, set back a little from the road in Dark Street Lane at the west end of Ridgeway. Walter's three older sisters, lifelong spinsters because of the deaths of young men in the First World War, lived their whole lives there.

The house had an enclosed yard and some out-buildings. In their boyhood and youth Walter's father used to pay him and his brothers a halfpenny each to wash down and tidy the yard every week. As time passed the three boys asked for a pay rise to a penny. Mr Pearse senior refused the increase. His sons went on strike. Old Mr Pearse again refused their claim and would not negotiate. Later he took them back – for a time on a lower wage of a farthing.

Walter served in the First World War. He was seriously injured in the last months of hostilities. He lost a lung and was lucky to survive. Not all the shrapnel could be removed and sixteen small pieces remained in him for the rest of his life. The injury plagued him, especially in his later years, causing him to lose his breath if he did too much. He learnt to live with it. He was a brave man.

In the 1920s, back from the Great War, he began to court Nancy, taking her to tennis parties at houses around Plympton. When he and Mum became friends, although she remained in awe of him, she told him how good-looking he had been in those days. He was '*dashing*', she said, dressed in his tennis whites.

'*He and his brother, Frank, were so handsome when I was young. They used to drive around the village in Walter's green sports car.*'

Walter was surprised by what Mum said and could not help being pleased to hear this. He had no pretence or vanity, and was honest and just, as well as firm and shrewd, both in business and personally. He was as steady as a rock. He became anxious only if he felt that there was a risk that he might not be able to honour what he had promised to do. His word was sacrosanct, and he expected others to keep their word, too.

There was a lighter, endearing side that we gradually got to know.

In the early morning in summer, still wearing pyjamas and a dark red silk dressing gown, Walter would take his first cup of tea into the back garden. We would hear him singing songs from musical comedies: 'This is My Lovely Day' from *Bless the Bride*, 'On the Street Where You Live' from *My Fair Lady*, 'People Will Say We're in Love' or 'Oh What a Beautiful Morning' from *Oklahoma!* and, most delightfully and incongruously, 'I Feel Pretty' from *West Side Story*.

Mum began to pass in to Walter and Nancy her daily newspaper. She used to write a few words to them each morning. 'Let's see what our Mrs Symons has got to say today,' Nancy used to say to Walter at breakfast. Then, in the summer, Mum would cut a rose from her overgrown back garden and in September a pear or two from Dad's pear tree, and leave them on the doormat with the paper. In return, Walter sometimes slipped Mum a large block of Cadbury's whole-nut chocolate, for which he and Nancy knew her taste.

As if in memory of their early days on the tennis court, both of them would watch every match at the Wimbledon tennis championship on television in June each year.

Walter was a man of deep, kindly feelings, and was perhaps more moved by sentiment than he realised. Although they were well off, he and Nancy always stayed on in the terraced house where they had made their home in 1929. The terrace had the best position in the village, he said, on fairly high ground, looking west down a gentle slope towards the afternoon and evening sun. There were glorious sunsets, reflecting the light on the sea four or five miles away.

Walter and Nancy were occasional churchgoers at St Mary's. In hospital, Mum said to me, '*I can see him now, in his tweed*

*suit, with a sprig of daphne odora in his buttonhole, going off to church
with Nancy on Easter Sunday.'*

Nancy's last years were difficult. She became disabled by
arthritis, and suffered a poor hip replacement operation. *'I had
a long chat with Mr Pearse... He and Mrs Pearse are fed up because
she is very closed in and cannot walk. He was glad to have a talk.'*
Not long before she died Nancy invited Mum in to Number 8
for coffee. In those days she and Walter used to give Mum little
presents, including *'a dear little dustbin. I used black bags for my
rubbish'*. Walter had been worried because Mum was putting
out all the rubbish together in a bag at the end of the week,
even in the bad weather that winter. He was afraid that she
would slip and used to telephone to check that she was well
when there was snow. *'I saw a dustbin in the garden and thought
that the dustbin-men were giving me a present at first. How soppy can
I get? The Pearses are dears.'*

Nancy died in December 1986, just before Walter's eighty-
eighth birthday. He arranged for her grave to be sited on the
right-hand side at the top of the steps leading to the upper
church yard, with the simple inscription, 'B A (Nancy) Pearse'
and her dates. He was devoted to her. Once, delivering Mum a
bar of chocolate, he brought out from under his pullover an old
photograph of Nancy hidden there to protect it from the rain
that morning. 'What do you think of that?' he asked Mum,
proud of Nancy's youthful good looks.

*'It is sad here with Mrs Pearse gone. It was nice of Jill to come
in when they are so worried and tell me that Mr Pearse will stay. I love
talking to him over the garden fence, even if he tells me when to go!
I hope that this won't knock the stuffing out of him: sixty-seven years
together is a great deal.'*

In the summer Walter would sometimes cut Mum's grass
when she was poorly or away visiting us, and she would do the
same for him. He once told her, 'I'm thinking of having a row
with you because you do too much for everyone.' Mum replied,
'If you did that I would move house.'

After Nancy's death I began to look in on Walter whenever

I visited Mum. One day he took down from his bookshelf the latest in his long series of five-year diaries and read me a laconic list of all the serious ailments from which Nancy had suffered in recent years, as if in tribute to her courage.

To Mum's surprise, Walter developed something of the same attitude of admiration towards her. He told her openly several times that he regarded her as a 'saint' because of all that she had done for Dad for so long during his illness. He said the same thing to me more than once. *'Mr Pearse said he tells everyone that I am an angel. Ha! Ha!'* Mum was embarrassed and amused, and she told him that it was nonsense to say that, but she was touched by his words nonetheless.

Mum and Walter began to speak quite frankly to each other. Mum dared to tell Walter that in our early days at Number 10 she had been afraid of him. Walter could not believe it at first and was shocked. She also told him of the day when he had thrown some conkers over the wall into our back garden and had hit her, painfully, on the head. We boys must have thrown them into his garden in the first place when we were playing. Mum relished the look on Walter's face when she told him this story; she liked to remind him of it.

Walter took Mum in his car to visit Kathleen Short after she had moved to the nursing home at Hooe where she spent her last years. It was the last time the three of them were all together. Afterwards Mum walked into Hooe churchyard to visit the grave of her brother Arthur, and then Walter took Mum for a wonderful drive through the lanes, ending at Saltram House. *'Mr Pearse is ever so funny and made me laugh.'*

Walter knew all the farmers around Plympton.

One hot August day Mum was seeing off a visitor when she noticed a man *'sitting on our front garden wall. I went over to ask him if he was all right. He asked for water and I got him some. He is a diabetic and lives on a farm at Shaugh. Anyway, the other day the bell rang and there he was. He had come to thank me for "saving his life", he said, and had brought me four books he had written about Dartmoor. I asked him in for a cup of tea and he stayed for two hours.*

Anyhow, I was not going to read the books (they are typewritten as it was too expensive to have them published) but when I opened one I couldn't put it down. It was all about his life at Shaugh and was really killing. I laughed all through it. People that I knew were mentioned and it was interesting. He knows Mr Pearse and Mr Short.

'*Pearsie said that he is eccentric. His name is Ernie Edwards and he had five brothers, all farmers except one who ran the mill at Loughtor Mill. He told me that he was a singer, a baritone, but no one will play the piano for him! He is eighty-one years old and, eccentric or not, I am grateful to him for making me laugh all the way through the books.*'

Three years later '*Mr Edwards was sitting on the front wall when I came out from visiting Kathleen. I went to ask him in for a cup of tea. He said,* "No, thank you. I don't want to trouble you as I didn't know that you were *'gentry'*. I saw your husband was a Major and had the M.B.E. in the telephone book so I can't bother you now that I know that you're gentry." *I said, "Don't be silly. I'm not gentry," so in he came and stayed an hour, waiting for the Shaugh bus and had tea and biscuits. He had been to his lawyer about his will. When I told him that I'd just returned from London, he said,* "So you've been to see the Queen?" *I said "No; my son and daughter-in-law." Isn't he funny?*'

Finally, a year later '*Mr Edwards came when Fred was here. I answered the door and he walked right out to the kitchen and sat down. It was very funny. I gave him tea and a piece of bread and cheese. Then I took him over the road to catch the bus. He asked me to go to Germany with him. Ha! Ha! Mr Pearse will be amused.*'

Mum enjoyed talking about incidents like this with Walter. They talked about old Plympton, and their love of it, and this shared enthusiasm made them allies. By then there was so little left of the old village, but it filled their memories and affections.

Both of them were interested in the famous Plympton hot cross bun, made on Good Friday. The buns had originally been baked in a shop in Dark Street Lane, near Barncott, but well before the Second World War they had been transferred to

Harry Stevens' bakery at the corner of Ridgeway and Moorland Road. In the early hours of Good Friday, a day on which in those years there was no other commercial activity, crowds of people used to walk from Plymouth and the nearby villages, to converge on Ridgeway to buy them. On their way they would gather bunches of primroses in the lanes to have ready to celebrate Easter Sunday.

Mum told Walter of a verse that she always claimed was traditional:

> 'The old Plympton bun is known far and wide
> From the banks of the Plym to the far Tamar side;
> The original baker is with us no more,
> But the buns are still baked in the South Devon store.'

In return, Walter passed on to Mum the secret part of the recipe, handed to him by a local dairy farmer. This explained the characteristic yellow colour that Harry Stevens' buns shared with those of the fabled 'original baker'. It was Channel Island milk, for which the farmer kept a small herd of Jersey cattle.

Towards the end of his life, Walter told me insistently and repeatedly that he really did regard Mum as some sort of saint. He spoke these words urgently to me. Perhaps he was keen to impress on me how lucky we were. Mum's strenuous denials and confusion had not changed his mind. It was as if Walter was puzzled and searching after whatever it was that had made it possible for Mum to live in the way that he so respected. There was something completely sincere, heartfelt and touching in this tribute. It showed how much two people of completely different temperament and experience had come to value and esteem each other.

On her eighty-eighth birthday, in hospital, Mum was talking to me about Walter. She had six months still to live. She had received many birthday cards, and the nurses had sung 'Happy Birthday'.

'*It's a good job the nurses are all so lovely,*' she said. '*They'll live to make the world a better place. This is a lovely ward...*'

Then, out of the blue, she added, '*Mr Pearse wasn't a lion. He was a lamb.*'

10

A Pattern
of Life

THERE WAS A PATTERN to our life in those years. I had
the feeling that it would never end, neither for Mum nor for
Judy and me.

If it is not possible to have children when you want them
(and we believed we should not do so because of the fifty-fifty
risk of my handing on Huntington's), the passing of time is
less visible, more hypnotic, more deceptive. Our childlessness
somehow gave me an experience of infinity or even eternity.
Judy looked no older as year succeeded year. Perhaps it was all
a dream; perhaps one day we would find that children could
safely come, or even that they had come, with all their games
and fun and pains, and then time, real time, would begin, and
begin to rush forwards.

Today as I set off for work from our house in London, I was
back in those days, so long ago. Through the window of a house
down the road I caught a glimpse of three little boys sitting at
table, waiting patiently for their mother or father to bring them
breakfast before they walked together to school. It is a rare
sight, full of cosiness and comfort. My heart turned. I had felt
that they were good parents and this proved it. Breakfast
together proved it. Perhaps we could have been like that. Who
can tell?

Such dreams somehow lived on in my heart and calmed those years. It was the time of my life, perhaps the time of our lives. It lasted about ten years.

Mum began to visit Judy and me in London after she had lost Rusty. Three times a year she came to stay with us. In time the visits fell back to two a year, then one, and finally, nearly twenty years later, they ceased altogether when *'Anno Domini'* took control, as Mum put it.

Mum travelled light. Her belongings would be folded into a small mustard-coloured hold-all, bought in Ridgeway for £5. I would collect her at Paddington station on a Saturday after-noon in our Morris Minor 1000 and bring her home across London, trying to make the trip interesting: through Hyde Park, past the Serpentine, and along the edge of The Green Park, with a glimpse of Buckingham Palace, through St James's Park and past Big Ben and the Houses of Parliament, over the River Thames, and then quickly down the Old Kent Road and through New Cross to Lewisham. In those years the traffic on Saturday was often light and we used to have a clear run.

Judy would greet us. We would have tea beside the fire, the table laid with a patterned violet cloth, brought out especially for these Saturday afternoons. We would use the silver teapot and fine bone china, in Art Deco style, that Judy's mother had received as a wedding-present in 1934.

Mum settled herself in the spare bedroom. On her bedside table she put a little leather wallet of photographs that she always carried in her handbag. In it there was a holiday snap of Dad on Challaborough beach, in an open-necked shirt and a long-sleeved pullover and grey flannel trousers. Mum called this picture of him 'Contemplation'.* Opposite it was one of her with my brother and me, taken on holiday in the lane near the caravan.

---

*   It is on the front cover of *Stranger on the Shore.*

Between the photos were a few Bible texts, which she had cut out over the years, chosen from those printed day by day at the head of the personal column in the *Daily Telegraph*:

'If God be for us, who can be against us?' (St Paul, Letter to the Romans, viii, 31);

'Let not your hearts be troubled, neither let them be afraid' (St John's Gospel, xiv, 27); and

'Now the God of hope fill you with all joy and peace in believing, that you may abound in hope' (St Paul, Letter to the Romans, xv, 13.)

Mum worked on the crossword by the fire while Judy put the finishing touches to our first supper together. She enjoyed everything, except chicken fricassee *('a waste of good ingredients, I call it')* although she sometimes mistook what she was eating *('Very nice, this rabbit,'* she said one evening, half way through a chicken casserole). She and I did the washing up; one day she poured away a bowl of an especially good soup that Judy was concocting.

Occasionally Mum travelled up from home on a Friday. She enjoyed the excitement of arriving at Paddington station in the rush hour. Once she came a week early. She was proud that, in her late sixties, she had found her way across London, by tube and Southern Region train, and arrived safely at our house. Aghast, we recognised her tall, stocky form and the colours of her dark green and brown tweed winter coat and brown hat through the glass panels in the front door. *'Mother!'* exclaimed Judy. She wanted to go home the next day but we persuaded her to stay.

On her return to Devon, Mum told her friends of her great adventure. Her pride was punctured by her old friend, Mary Bassett, the cub leader and doctor's receptionist, who retorted, 'Well, you've got a tongue in your' ade, haven't you, Grace?'

When in April 1980 Jumble, a border terrier, entered our life, Mum's visits were transformed. For the first few months we also had Sam, Jumble's brother. *'There are two little dogs just like Jumble and Sam running down the middle of Thornwood Road,'* Mum called out to us on the evening on which she had arrived. Somehow Jumble and Sam had managed to slip out under the garden gate. Mum took care of them like gold-dust while we were in France for a week. A few weeks later we lost Sam to the canine parvovirus, a new disease that became virulent among dogs at that time.

Three times a day Mum took Jumble to Manor House Gardens, our local park. There she had long conversations with some of the regular dog-walkers: Joan, wearing a woolly hat in winter, faithfully walking with Rex, whatever the weather – she was known as 'Mrs Rex' to the local shopkeepers; Cyril, the friendly retired dustman, with his dog, Judy; Marjorie, with her cavalier spaniel, Tina; and Doris and her husband Cyril, who took it in turns to walk their cocker spaniel, Andy.

Mum made friends with our neighbours in Thornwood Road, many of them of about her age. They shared their memories of the country before the Second World War. Mum enjoyed hearing from them of the romance and excitement of life in London in those distant days when she and Wally had visited Uncle Jack and Auntie Nellie.

Opposite us at Number 29 lived Doris and Fred. Fred had worked as a commercial traveller. In retirement, he took up painting and produced an accurate and poignantly heartfelt watercolour of our house, the view that he and Doris had looked out on for all their married life, now with our Morris Minor standing in front of it.

Next door to us, at Number 26, were Henry and Liliana, with their six children. They entertained Mum with stories of life in the Army. Henry had worked as a chef in the Army Catering Corps at several bases on the Continent.

At Number 24 lived John and Marion, his invalid wife. John told Mum about his work in London docks where he had spent many years. He spun vivid, racy stories of his childhood on the Isle of Dogs, two generations before the docks became Docklands, in the style of Manhattan.

Finally, at Number 20, were John and May, a Roman Catholic couple from Londonderry. They told Mum about the 1930s in Ulster, many happy stories of cheerful, good relations between Protestants and Catholics, paradoxical to us at a time of renewed conflict in Northern Ireland. John told her how much he, as a boy, and his family had enjoyed the Protestant bands and processions in those days. Later, when John was widowed, he used to talk to Mum about his loss and his memories of May, whose grave he visited every day.

For these neighbours and the dog-walking companions in the park, Mum's visits to us came to be like the periodic return of the swallow. She would call on them each time to say goodbye before going back to Plympton.

We used to take Mum to a play at the Greenwich Theatre, thriving at that time under the leadership of Ewan Hooper and, after him, Alan Strachan. They achieved their great success by making demands of their audience. They devised a programme for both highbrow and middlebrow tastes, for example, Goldoni's *Artful Widow,* Wilde's *Ideal Husband* and *A Woman of No Consequence,* and, by way of contrast, Sophocles' *Oedipus* plays. Most powerful of all, on a frosty winter's evening, was the performance of Euripides' *Trojan Women,* which we saw from the back row of the theatre, enthralled in a still, deep silence.

On Saturday we might take Mum for a drive in the country in Kent and East Sussex. We visited the garden at Sissinghurst Castle. Mum resisted the temptation to take cuttings. After a walk around the garden, we bought fish and chips at the shop in the village and ate them in the Castle car park, attended by a robin and chaffinch.

We might take her for a walk at Ide Hill, near Sevenoaks. Before the great storm of October 1987 the hill was crowned by a massive stand of beech trees. Below them to the south lay many acres of oak, ash and hornbeams where Jumble chased rabbits. In May there was a sea of bluebells. We had lunch by the fire in the village pub. Mum relished observing how the customers tackled their food (*'that woman ate two pies, and, boy, did she enjoy them!'*). Then we went home to the fireside at Number 28, with a cup of tea, and perhaps a final walk with Jumble in Manor House Gardens.

On Sunday, Mum came with us to our local church for the service of Holy Communion. Sometimes we all went to Evensong.

In her hold-all Mum brought her well-worn blue Bible, and with it the prayers written on scraps of paper slipped in between its pages. She would make her prayers night and morning, and sometimes on the landing upstairs I would hear the quiet murmur of her saying them.

The days raced past. All the things that we could not normally do because we were out at work all day, we would find done for us when we got home in the evening. All my woollen socks would be beautifully darned, and Mum would do some weeding in the garden.

After Peggy's death in 1975 Judy missed out on the pleasure of visits that her mother would have made to stay with us. Perhaps her awareness of this made Mum even more grateful for the warm welcome Judy gave her.

In hospital, Judy was often in Mum's thoughts, happy thoughts and full of good memories.

'I've always loved Judy,' she told me. *'She's a godsend in an earthquake. Thank her for being a lovely daughter to me. She knows what to do in a predicament. Who can help loving her?'*

The time would come for Mum to return home. At Paddington we bought her a copy of *Country Life* to read on the journey. If she left on a Saturday or Sunday, we settled her down in the first-class carriage where, for paying a one-pound supplement, she could travel on her second-class ticket.

If she left on a weekday, Judy used to take her to Paddington. I could sometimes slip out of the office at lunch-time and get there to see her off. I would arrive on the platform in my office suit. Mum's eyes would light up. 'I know what you are thinking,' Judy said to her, and when she got home Mum wrote, '*You looked so fine and smart out there on the platform and I was indeed just as proud as Judy thought!*'

Mum loved those rail journeys. Once, as she travelled through Berkshire, she saw a kingfisher – a flash of blue and burnt orange along the surface of the canal. She told us of her conversations at various times with a nun, an actress and, often, young people.

Back at Number 10 she would thirstily enjoy her first full cup of tea for the day. She knelt in the kitchen by the Rayburn in order to light its oil burner. Occasionally Kathleen would come in from next door to see Mum.

Before she got into bed that night Mum wrote a short entry in her diary. '*John and Judy took me to Paddington… Very sad am I… Week in London restored me.*' On another occasion she wrote, '*Lovely to be back in **Dad's** house.*'

And to us she wrote, '*I was very sad to leave Jumble. He did not like it when I brought my bag downstairs. It was lovely to see you at Paddington, John. Thank you for* Country Life *and for helping me onto the train. I felt quite a snob reading that when most people had* The Sun. *Thank you both for Ide Hill woods and the pub lunches and also, Judy, for the good grub at no. 28. I cannot help smiling at the thought of my visit cheering you up. I am not the gay bird that I used to be! I am quite a moaner now. I think you will be glad to see the back of me. It is good of you to ask me. I enjoyed being with you and it was good of you, Judy, to fetch me at Paddington. I thought your house and garden lovely, and I feel very much at home with you. Don't let that frighten you.*'

11

Time Passes

CHRISTMAS GAVE MUM joy to the end of her life. It was a devotion that went back to her earliest days: *'Our house was filled with holly and ivy, and we just had stockings filled with simple presents, and oranges, apples, and nuts. We had a lovely Christmas dinner and Christmas pudding (set alight with brandy), with ten of us around the table.'*

Mum loved the frantic atmosphere in the shops as everyone stocked up for the holidays. As long as her bachelor brothers Jack and George were alive, she made them a massive fruit cake, a plum pudding and a dozen mince pies. These she delivered to Number 7 on Christmas Eve when they kept open house there for family and friends.

Over the decades her diaries record:

'23rd November started puddings';

'1st December made mincemeat.'

Each Christmas Eve we would take Mum to Hooe parish church, opposite the house where Arthur had died on Boxing Day. She would clamber out of the car and carry a wreath of holly to his grave and for a few minutes experience the silence with him there.

After a while we would drive up to the cliffs overlooking Plymouth Sound and gaze at the waters within and beyond the breakwater which made it such a safe harbour, and in the distance the elegant terraces of houses on Plymouth Hoe.

One Boxing Day the three of us went to Burrator Reservoir for a walk across the dam and in the surrounding woods. We ended the outing with a Williams's dairy ice-cream cornet or wafer, smeared with Devonshire clotted cream. It was unexpectedly mild that year, and the Williams's van had been tempted out. With a wafer, there was a special joy in the last few bites: nothing but the wafer biscuits soaked in ice-cream, with a rich layer of almost gritty cream between them.

In the weeks before the first of her three Christmases in hospital, Mum said to me,

'Everyone wants to be at home for Christmas …

'It's lovely to be at home at Christmas.'

Perhaps she was hoping even then to get home to Number 10 and spend Christmas there. It could not be.

We often spent Easter with Mum, too.

In Holy Week in 1975, on Maundy Thursday, we took Mum and Auntie Florrie to Weir Quay. It is a quiet spot on the River Tamar, which forms the border between Devon and Cornwall, hidden away just north of where the River Tavy joins it.

Ten years had passed since Uncle Charlie had died. Hurrying home to Florrie after his last day's work on the railway, he had been run over and killed by a railway engine before he could enjoy his retirement.

The sky was blue, with small clouds and almost no wind. There was a freshness in the air. Mum and Florrie sat, in their tweed coats and warm hats, on a green wooden bench beside the river. Judy and I watched them from downstream as we had a walk. They drank cups of tea from the thermos, and ate Mum's chocolate Madeira cake. They talked in their usual animated way, mixing laughter and some sad memories from the old days.

Mum had her binoculars on her lap. She loved bird-watching. At that time the huge estates which now spread there had not been built at Torridge and Chaddlewood. Many varieties of bird still visited Mum's front and back gardens. Thrushes nested in the wisteria by her front door; coal-tits came, greenfinches by the dozen, nuthatches, marsh-tits and willow-tits, chaffinches, tree creepers, wrens and robins. Blue tits nested in the green nesting box opposite the kitchen window and brought up a family: in Mum's words *'tiny balls of blue and yellow fluff hopping up the back garden path on the day that they fledged.'*

On Easter Sunday we went to the eight o'clock service at St Mary's church with Mum and met all the regulars. After the service we walked up to the churchyard and visited Dad's grave, with its granite headstone near the boundary hedge. A robin sang. We sensed Dad with us. We tidied the grave a little, and put some flowers in a jam-jar by the headstone.

Mum told me that she wished her ashes to be laid there, with Dad, *'slipped into the grave so as not to disturb him'.*

This was a change of heart. In her middle years Mum had not liked the idea of cremation. Wally and Audrey had some-times taken her for an outing to Mothecombe beach at the mouth of the River Erme. Once, Auntie Hilda and Uncle Fred were there, too. With the sea sparkling in the sun and the laughter of children calling out to each other as they played in the water, Audrey turned to Hilda and asked her, *'Hilda, do you want to be cremated?'*

Mum loved St Mary's church, partly for all the memories of her wedding and many other family events, partly for its link with so many of her friends over a lifetime, and partly for the vicars and curates whom she had seen come and go.

In her handbag Mum kept a visiting-card left by Mr Mitchell, the vicar during the Second World War, when he had called on her at Number 7, Stone Barton before she left for

India with me in January 1946. *'Called to see Mother and Baby, but found you out,'* Mr Mitchell had written in pencil, much faded over the years, but greatly treasured and often handled by Mum.

Mr Mitchell was coming up to retirement in 1954 when the Tory Brook was so swollen by persistent rain on Dartmoor that it overflowed its banks and swept through the church. A photograph in the local newspaper showed him picking up prayer-books floating in the floodwater in the aisle.

After Mr Mitchell came Mr Wackett, a former schoolmaster, an efficient, cheerful man and a good preacher of short sermons. He had the manner of a padre and was famously popular for going, in his dog-collar, to drink a pint of beer at the Colebrook Inn after Matins on Sunday mornings.

The next vicar was Mr Matthews, who stayed for twenty years. At the end of his time, by when he had been widowed, the church became rather rundown. *'A lady told me that she couldn't hear Mr Matthews and that she would not come back. His voice is now weak and it is difficult. Last Sunday evening I went to Evensong. We sang 'The Lord is My Shepherd', my mother's favourite hymn, but even so there is a lot missing at St Mary's: three clergy but no feeling of fellowship.'*

A month later hope returned. *'There were a nice lot of young people in church on Sunday evening. I have a feeling that people will come back to the church, as it used to be.'*

In 1983, Mr Richards arrived and brought a breath of fresh air. In November of that year Mum wrote in her diary, *'Mr Richards' first service. Church full: awe-inspiring.'*

At about that time Mum was amused by the novels of Barbara Pym, so many of which recorded incidents in the heroines' lives involving curates in London churches in the 1950s. Perhaps the role of curates in Plympton in the 1970s and 1980s was not all that different from what Miss Pym had observed in the suburbs of London thirty years earlier.

Mum came to know especially well one of Mr Matthews' curates, Peter Morgan, who was unusually 'High' for Plympton

St Mary's and performed complex rituals at services. *'We have an unusual curate at St Mary's,'* Mum wrote to me. *'He is very High Church... He has a lovely clear voice.'*

'I will be having the curate to call soon. He swaggered along yesterday and called out, "Coming to see you soon." They say that he stays two hours. He travels around in a Mexican-type black hat and cape, and everyone in the shops seems to like him; quite a character. He sweeps off his hat to every lady.'

Some of the congregation did not get used to Peter Morgan and his elaborate rituals. Mum was not 'High', but she was happy to take him as she found him. He did visit her, *'and we had a very interesting conversation. He is a very kind man indeed.'*

Mum went on to enjoy many talks with him. Usually they met at the front gate when she was gardening and he was on his way to visit the shops or to take his letters to the post office. Mum once found him sitting on her garden wall, faint from the heat, like Ernie Edwards the farmer before him. She invited him into the house for a spoonful of brandy, which she kept for occasions when she felt 'squawmish'.

On another occasion, after visiting an old people's home, Mr Morgan told her about it and then shuddered and said, *'Disgusting.'* Despite her own advanced age, Mum found his honesty refreshing and highly amusing. *'He's a funny chap and he makes me laugh.'* Mum dreaded the possibility of becoming, as she put it, an 'inmate' of such an institution: *'I hope to avoid it a little longer. When I lose my determination, I shall be ready for "Dickie's Meadow".'*

A little later Mr Morgan married a Plympton girl, Ruth, a member of the church choir. The first sign that something was afoot was that Mr Morgan *'lost four stone'*. He took Ruth to meet his parents: *'We are all keyed up regarding this romance.'* Mum attended the wedding service.

Peter Morgan was as good a priest as he was a source of good humour. He showed that in 1982 when Mum was alone at Easter.

The Argentinians had invaded the Falkland Islands, British territory, on Good Friday, the second of April. Mum's shock at the wanton, unprovoked attack became mixed with her religious feelings, prompted by Holy Week, and unsettled her. *'Cried much,'* she wrote in her diary. She enjoyed the Easter services, but was very upset again on the following Tuesday. Peter Morgan visited her for a talk. In her diary Mum recorded around this time of Mr Morgan, *'He spoke to me very kindly,'* and again that *'he called for a chat'*. *'I have a great liking for him,'* she told me.

A few days later Judy and I arrived for a weekend visit. Mum continued to be worried by the Falklands War. She recorded her fears and hopes:

'Bad news: two more losses,' on the seventh of May;

'Better news,' on the twelfth;

'Better news,' again on the twenty-ninth; and

'War over... white flag raised; great rejoicing; sad loss of life,' on the fourteenth and fifteenth of June.

Gradually, Mum regained her equilibrium during the summer. She was shaken when the press and the BBC raked over the campaign. We talked about it. *'On reflection,'* she wrote to me, *'I made a mistake. Our forces were marvellous and they stood up well for the poor islanders.'*

She recalled what she had written at Whitsun in 1980 when, again after Mrs Thatcher authorised the action, the SAS had saved the lives of hostages taken by revolutionary fanatics in the Iranian Embassy. *'The last few days have been dramatic at the siege, with the wonderful work of the SAS and the police. It could only happen in our country. It is good to be British. It could help the American hostages at their Embassy in Teheran, as we all hope.'*

Not long after their marriage, the Morgans left Plympton for a parish in North Devon. During a talk at the front gate, Peter Morgan told Mum, *'The people of Plympton are in for a shock and some changes in their services when Mr Matthews retires as vicar.'*

Roger Beck took over from Mr Morgan. Mum got to know him best of all the curates, especially in her last years.

In India Dad had admired the work of the British and Foreign Bible Society. He and Mum supported the Society's work for the rest of their lives. A representative of the Society happened to live near them and Mum got to know his wife, Mrs Sandford, who took her on an adventure.

'*She took me hell-for-leather in her car up to Cornwood to Dr Bussell's house and then ordered me to ring the big bell hanging outside the cottage. "I want you to ring that bell **very loudly**." I foolishly did so, and incurred Mrs Bussell's wrath. She came out and asked, "What do you think you are doing?" She had no idea who Mrs Sandford was. You see, she was having a breakdown and I didn't know about it. Then she drove me back home at great speed. Mr Sandford was so worried. When I think about it all now, I find it very funny, but not at the time. She is fine now, and I miss seeing them now that they have moved. We used to have good talks. Mrs Sandford used to call my old-fashioned upright buns "right-ups".*'

After they moved from Plympton to Clifton, the Sandfords used to send Mum a Christmas letter. It meant a lot to her. In 1995 Mr Sandford wrote Mum a wonderful letter, brave and full of faith, which began, 'It may be that this will be the last letter that you will receive from me at Christmas, after all these years...' '*I do hope that he is not in too much pain,*' Mum wrote, when she passed us the news of his illness. Six months later she saw the notice of his death in the paper.

Until her late seventies Mum came with us on good walks. She and Judy would make a picnic, with pasties or sandwiches, fruit and an old blue thermos full of hot water for tea and coffee. We would gather together rugs and coats and hats, and, with Jumble, we would set off for the Devon countryside.

One of her favourites started at Plymbridge and followed the footpath up the course of the old branch-line railway from Marsh Mills junction beside the River Plym. Dad and Mum had taken us on an outing by train on that line to Yelverton and Princetown.

As we walked by the river Mum told us that she and her brother Jack had once seen a salmon jump out of the water and land on the low-lying gravel bank. They had wrapped it in dock leaves and had taken it home. Their mother cooked it and made the sauces that she had been taught when she had been in service to the Prince of Wales and Princess Alexandra in the 1880s.

In summer we went to walk by the sea in the South Hams. We parked near the 'Journey's End' pub at Ringmore and walked down the steep footpath to Ayrmer cove, the 'Magic Beach' of our childhood holidays in the caravan at Challaborough. We had a swim, followed by chocolate cake and a cup of tea on a beach as deserted and beguiling as any visited by Odysseus on his wanderings, about which I had read, there by the sea, when I devoured Homer's works as a schoolboy.

After the picnic we walked back to the village and ate an ice-cream from the village shop, sitting in the graveyard of All Hallows church. With Dad's binoculars we looked out to sea and searched for the Eddystone lighthouse on the horizon. Then we drove back to Number 10 for a cup of tea in the back garden.

In the car on the way home we would sing one or two of Mum's pantomime songs:

> *'Mary Ellen at the church turned up;*
> *Her pa turned up*
> *And her ma turned up;*
> *Little brother Bert,*
> *Big sister Gert,*
> *Even the parson with his shirt turned up.*

'But no bridegroom with the ring turned up;
A telegram boy
With his nose turned-up;
The telegram said
He didn't want to wed;
And they found him in the river with his toes
*   turned-up.'*

After one of our trips, Mum wrote to Judy and me:

'You make my life complete,
Gee, but you're awfu' sweet ...'

Of course, the trouble with happy visits is that they come to an end.

Time was passing. Time also ends.

12

'Gone are the days...'

LIFE GREW HARDER for Mum.

Her old friends noticed the change. 'Fancy you ending up like this, Grace,' said one of those who had worked with her at Yeo's when they met at the shops in Ridgeway. *'You'm* still alive, then, Grace,' said another, in the broad Devon idiom. A third asked her, 'Are you or Wally the elder, Grace?' *'Rather flattering,'* she wrote to me.

Mum loved to joke with us about these comments, but things really were changing.

The population of Plympton had grown to twenty-four thousand by 1985, and was still growing. When the city of Plymouth achieved the ambition that it had long nursed of extending eastwards, it smothered Plympton. The life and identity of an ancient Devonshire village were at risk of being rubbed out. Some of the arrivals tried to hold on to the way of life that had attracted them in the first place but Plympton and, with it, Moorland Road became less peaceful.

Uncle George's health had been growing worse for years, especially the varicose ulcers on his legs and feet. He found it impossible to find comfortable shoes. Ingeniously, Mum made him a pair of size fourteen slippers from two felt hats.

George had been forced by his bad health to give up his fruit and vegetable stall in Plymouth Market in 1974 when he was seventy-two, much sooner than he had wished. He sold it for a good sum of money. *'Last week Uncle George was expecting to receive a cheque for £2,000 for the goodwill of the stall and will not be going to the market any more. I am very glad and maybe his foot will get a bit better at home. He is at the Crownhill nursing home, with physiotherapy three times a week. It is a new lease of life. I have been to visit him twice in the last week.'*

A year later Mum had to write to him that the money would run out if he continued to spend it lavishly. She was continuing the work of their brother Arthur in saving George from himself. Fred, who used to visit George every day before coming to Mum, told her that her words had an effect on him. *'George went very quiet when he read the letter. I am sorry to jolt him. Poor George, but I must not shirk my duty.'*

After Jack died in March 1976, Mum often visited George to clean the house and spend some time with him. *'I love it,'* she told me. She made him a steak-and-kidney pie. George said, 'It was the first I have eaten since Mother died in 1943.'

She came to understand the efforts that Jack had made to keep house for himself and George. *'Since I began working at Number 7 I have a close insight into Uncle Jack's character. He was pretty good in achieving what he did, and he was struggling against great odds. Jack had been poorly for some time before he died.'*

'I worried about George,' she told me. *'Was he looking after himself? Was he getting enough to eat? I imagined him eating bread and cheese and drinking tea, with his poor legs resting on a stool.'*

George did little housework, but he always cooked himself a good dinner. He never complained about his leg ulcers. Every so often Mum would walk to Stone Barton with a picnic of ham sandwiches to share with him, with cups of tea. She would clean the house. The task of washing the accumulated milk bottles, smeared and stained with rancid, congealed milk took a lot of effort. Before she left, she would proudly line them up on the doorstep, now shining and crystal-clear, perhaps twenty or thirty in all.

'It makes me feel better when I go there,' she told me as the years passed. *'He is as happy as ever, which makes me think that possessions do not make one happy.'* And, when Mum was seventy-three, she wrote to me, *'I worked hard, but we had a laugh or two. He never grumbles about his terrible legs... I felt great.'*

But by her seventy-fifth year Mum wrote, *'I regard going to George with increasing revulsion... However, the rewards are great... Poor old George kept thanking me; his legs were very painful. How he gets by is indeed a miracle.'*

For a while George began to improve. He did a bit of housework between Mum's visits. On a few occasions he even washed the dirty milk bottles and put them out on the doorstep for the milkman. *'George is putting the milk bottles out on the step. Success at last! He said to Fred, "When is Grace coming up? It's looking as good as Buckingham Palace here today!"'* But, as his legs got worse, Mum found blood which had oozed from his ulcers when she washed his sheets. Eventually he had to sleep on a chair with his legs up on a stool, which eased the pain.

'He is very disabled now, but very brave,' Mum told me.

A few months later, in December 1985, George died of a stroke. He was eighty-three years old. Mum and Fred organised the funeral. They cleared out Number 7, on which no real work had been done in the forty years since Mum had left it in January 1946 to join Dad in India, taking me with her.

The state of George's health and the spartan conditions in which he had lived preyed on Mum's mind for many months after his death.

'He could have had quite a different life if he had gone into the Army, but no one encouraged him. **If you don't have someone to encourage you, you don't bother.** *He used to keep all sad things under concrete blocks. But other people can't be responsible for you.*

'Everyone always wanted to help George. In hospital, after his stroke, all the nurses wanted to care for him. "I'll bath George," *they used to say.'*

It was only at midsummer that Mum recovered her spirits. *'I played the piano yesterday,'* she told me, *'The first time since George died.'*

Mum spoke to Wally or Audrey every day on the telephone. They occasionally took her out for a drive, until they gave up their car. The frequent contact could be a mixed blessing. *'George was much more jolly than they are,'* she said. When they took her on a trip in the sun to the moors near Cornwood, *'Their conversation was deeply depressing, as usual … I took all night and half of yesterday to get over it.'*

Mum made light of what was happening. She said she was afraid of becoming what her old friend Lily Coombes, in their youth, had called one of the older staff at Yeo's – *'a bitter weed'*.

Mum went on some wonderful drives with her nephew Jack and his wife Phyllis. One drive on Dartmoor brought back memories of her honeymoon. *'At Holne Chase I had a good look at Church Inn as Dad and I had bread and cheese and a Coxes apple there. He had a glass of beer and I had a glass of lemonade on our honeymoon. Very nostalgic! It was rationing days, of course, then.'*

Uncle Fred became ill in the late summer of 1987. In December he had to move into a residential home. It was difficult for him. Fred dearly loved his own home. During the Second World War he had sent a verse to Hilda from Germany, setting it to a tune of his own:

> *'Everybody loves their little home,*
> *And I love mine,*
> *It's so divine.*
> *I often wonder why I went to roam*
> *So far across the mighty foam.*
> *It matters not how long I've been away-*
> *Come home some day,*
> *I hope and pray-*
> *No one seems to grumble if it's rich or humble –*
> *Everybody loves their little home.'*

Mum became distressed that she could not do more for Fred. With a heavy heart she explained this to him. He understood. Mum wrote a tactful letter to John (his son) whose godmother she was, to explain the situation. John lived in the north of England. He and his wife, Margaret, began to visit Fred more frequently, which helped him.

Mr and Mrs Kelly, the old friends who kept the little, old-fashioned grocery shop in Ridgeway, retired at the end of 1988. The shop's new owners did not sell groceries.

In January 1990 Walter Pearse, who had gone to stay with his daughter and her family for Christmas, did not return. He nursed the hope that he might be able to return in the summer, but it was not to be.

In July 1990 Fred died. He had been unhappy in the home. Once during those two and a half years, Mum wrote, *'Fred actually smiled today.'* After his death Mum often recorded in her diary: *'I miss Fred.'*

Mum's visits to stay with us in London went down from three to two a year, and then to one. She stayed with us for the last time, both in London and at our cottage in East Sussex, at the end of May 1991. It was bluebell time. We walked slowly in the woods and enjoyed their colour and heady smell on the slope bordering the River Limden. On Bank Holiday Monday Mum managed to come to a barbeque party given by our neighbour. She hated barbeques, but gave them to believe that she had a wonderful time.

At the cottage Mum admired my work on the vegetable patch. *'I always said you would be happier hoeing turnips than doing anything else,'** she reminded me. *'It's a fine job, although people don't think so these days.'*

* She was on to something, as usual. I am never happier than when digging.

And she quoted,

> 'The cure for this ill is not to sit still,
> Or frowst with a book by the fire,
> But to take a large hoe and a shovel also,
> And dig till you gently perspire.'*

The following Wednesday Judy took her to Paddington for the last time to return to Plymouth. On the drive to the station she caught a final glimpse of the Serpentine where she had steered the boat erratically as Wally had rowed, sixty-five years earlier.

Kathleen Short died in October 1991. Mum had visited her in May, *'blind and alone and sitting in a corner'*. Mum quoted what Kathleen had sometimes said to her, *'Everything and everyone wears out.'*

In her will Kathleen bequeathed Mum her barometer; she left me Gordon's wing armchair.

In her twenty-three years at Number 10 after Dad's death Mum fed on the memories of what had made us all happy there over the years. She preserved the stories handed down within her family; what had been the first words of each of her brothers and sisters (her own had been, *'The flies will bite you'*; George's *'I know a bird's nest: four eggs – thrush's'*; Wally's *'Golly, golly, golly, golly...'*); family jokes; and comic and embarrassing incidents, often brought out with wicked glee and to telling effect, when nephews and nieces visited her with their spouses to whom the stories were new. She remembered the films that she had seen with her mother; the books she had read; and the words and tunes of songs that she had sung as a little girl at the pantomime each Christmas, as a sheet with the words painted on it was lowered above the stage.

---

* 'How the Camel got his Hump' from *Just So Stories* by Rudyard Kipling.

'*I try to accept old age gracefully and avoid being a bitter weed,*' she wrote to me.

'*I've had some great times... I used to see huge flocks of goldfinches in the fields by Parkstone Cottages on the way with the dogs to Newnham House... Dogs are so easy to live with...*

'*It's sad that one has to grow old before one can be free to wander...*

'*As Dad used to say*

> "Life is very sweet, brother;
> there is night and day, brother, both sweet things;
> sun, moon and stars, brother, all sweet things;
> there is likewise a wind on the heath,
> life is very sweet, brother."*

'*I look back on my visits to you in London when you used to take me to Ide Hill with Jumble, and the majestic ring of beech trees, and the sausage and chips and tomatoes at the Inn, and the viburnum growing in the hedge...*

'*I remember the journeys back to dear old Number 10 on the train, seeing the kingfisher on the canal in Wiltshire and all the primroses in the fields and hedges and railway embankments as we reached Devon...*

'*I am sad at not being with you on your birthday. It's difficult now that my legs are such a nuisance. I guess that my travelling days are coming to a close...*

'*All good things come to an end...*'

A few weeks later, just before her eighty-second birthday, Mum wrote to us again. '*This is a very sad letter for me, as I love to come to visit you in London and the cottage but it is no good. I cannot face the three- or four-hour journey... This letter is short, but I am sad.*'

On the same day in her diary she made a short note: '*John rang. He understands.*'

'*London can be very beautiful,*' she wrote to us later. '*I remember Judy taking me to the Serpentine in autumn on the way to*

---

* Based on words of George Borrow in *Lavengro*, Chapter 25, which were reproduced on a small water-colour of heather in flower on Dartmoor which hung beside the fireplace in the dining room at Number 10 for many years.

Paddington when huge leaves covered the ground. Jumble was rushing around chasing the leaves.'

The telephone became even more important to us. Judy would hear gales of laughter at my end of the line as she prepared our supper. There would be funny stories about odd incidents, or the quirky characters that Mum had met or observed going about their business in Ridgeway, or some comments made to her. But it was Mum's general attitude and humour rather than the jokes that caused the laughter. With the same temperament we knew at once what would help or encourage the other, especially laughter.

One evening on one of my visits we were sitting on opposite sides of the fireplace, reading. In those days of hope in the Soviet Union I used to read the Russian cultural paper, *'Literaturnaya Gazeta'*. Looking up and seeing me deep in its massive pages, bigger than the biggest English broadsheet newspaper, Mum said, earnestly, *'I don't know you.'* I knew exactly what she meant. How we laughed about it. Those who know us best and wish us best are, perhaps, most willing to accept that their knowledge, though great, is limited.

When she reached eighty-three years, Mum could get to St Mary's only when we were staying with her. She was afraid to accept the lifts that the other 'eight- o'clockers' offered her, in case she caught her bad leg on the door of a strange car.

At first she also turned down the clergy's offer to celebrate the Holy Communion for her at home. It would have meant that she had accepted that her old way of life was over and done with, and that she would never get to church again. But, at last, she agreed when Roger Beck suggested that he should come on a Wednesday afternoon once a month and celebrate the service with her. Mum came to love those occasions. Roger would spread a little white cloth on her side-table near the fireplace in the sitting-room, and would place on it a lighted candle, her prayer-book, together with a small Communion chalice for the wine and a patten for wafers. Afterwards Mum and Roger would sit by the fire for a while and talk.

In November 1993 Wally died. *'It is all very sad, and poor Audrey does not realise anything at times,'* Mum wrote after the funeral. By the next summer Audrey was much better. *'I have just had a beautiful card from Audrey, and inside it was a dear message. She has now come back from Bournemouth and has had a lovely time. I am so glad.'* With the help of her sons and daughter-in-law Audrey was able to visit Mum from time to time, and she went on to outlive her by a few years.

A month after Wally's death Walter Pearse followed him. After he had moved away to live with his daughter, he and Mum had often talked on the telephone. She had forwarded all his post to him. She and Betty, who had cooked and helped Walter and Nancy faithfully for many years, had kept a careful watch over his house. In this way Mum had felt he was still next door.

Walter bequeathed to Mum the Victorian wrought-iron garden seat on which they had often sat together and talked.

The following February Mum came on a short walk with me in the pathfields leading to St Maurice. We took a thermos with us. We found the first celandines shining at the foot of the lime trees planted there to celebrate Queen Victoria's diamond jubilee. We watched a wren and a robin building their nests in the hedge by the slate wall. We knew that this would be Mum's last real walk, in a spot that she had always loved. A man and his wife, passing through the pathfields to the shops in Ridgeway, took a photograph of us sitting on the bench as we drank a cup of coffee. Mum became more or less housebound but was still able to take care of herself there with help from Betty and her husband Glen.

When we visited Mum, we found ourselves doing more and more to help her to keep going between visits. Mum hated our 'working for her' (as she put it) but the thought of leaving Number 10, where she had lived for so long with Dad, was anathema to her. Every night she used to say 'goodnight' to him, stepping into the enormous cupboard under the stairs, and gently touching his last trilby hat, still hanging on one of the pegs there. These memories and associations kept her going.

'Getting up is a slow business, but I get there in the end. Today I rose at 6.30 and have just finished breakfast at 10.30.'

In her own mind, Mum was ready for death. She loved life. She felt that she was lucky in her family and friends, but I now know better than I then did how much pain and loneliness she suffered in her last ten years. After all that she had been through during Dad's illness, I hoped that she would have a quick and easy end.

Mum did not fear death. She feared judgement, but she knew that beyond judgement lies God's mercy, each somehow giving meaning to the other. She had a strong sense that life continued through death.

In her last couple of years at Number 10, Mum had two unusual experiences, which puzzled her. She did not make much of them. To me, it seemed that she was living somehow in the borderland between this world and the next. We were to find ourselves spending a lot of time together in those regions.

On the first of these two occasions, Mum was in bed. It was as if her mother were in the bedroom with her, standing over her. Mum reached up to kiss her and said, *'Don't worry.'* Puzzled and a little alarmed at what was happening, Mum switched on the light. She did not know whether it was a dream or some other sort of experience that she had never had before. She told me that it had felt quite different from the dream that she had had the previous night, about her mother and father and her seven brothers and sisters, all together at Number 7, Stone Barton.

On the second occasion, Mum was sitting in her armchair beside the fire in the sitting-room. She had a dream in which she and my brother were in the kitchen by the Rayburn. Suddenly, Dad came down the stairs, fit and well, dancing and singing, and we all joined in the dance.

In the days at 'Babworth', our bungalow at St Ives, wearing his old corduroy trousers and pullover and trilby hat, Dad used to lead us in a dance through the bungalow and around the garden, past the tulips and wallflowers and, later, in the summer, the lupins which did so well there. Dad would sing and we would join in.

Mum awoke, and she had a continuing strong sensation that Dad was in the chair at the other side of the fireplace, where he always used to sit, next to the piano.

Mum saw the funny side of things.

'Just finished my breakfast at 12 noon, after getting up at ten to seven and having my bath...Why does it take me so long to bath? Answer: Anno Domini.'

In another letter she wrote, *'It was funny using the mop under my bed at three a.m. to find my false teeth ...'*

In April 1994 Mum passed out when she was sitting at the kitchen table after breakfast. Her old friends Nan Matthews and Betty Peters realised that something was amiss and saved her life. In hospital it was discovered that she needed an operation, which took place in September.

Judy took a week's leave from school in October and looked after her when she came home after her stay in hospital. After their week together, Mum wrote,

'Judy spoiled me ...

'I miss Judy ...

'I'm here at Number 10. Thanks be to God.'

She wrote to us, *'Simple pleasures are the best of all. I will endeavour to accept things gracefully, and am sorry to worry you ... I will not deny that I like being here in this house. The sun is shining, the sky is blue, the garden and house are tidy, I have had a good breakfast by the Rayburn and there is a lovely late rose on the window sill.'*

Mum made a good recovery and did give in about some things. We went there for Christmas, but this time we did most of the work. We made the Christmas puddings according to her recipe, written down for us in 1991 when we first did it together:

> *3 lbs each of washed raisins, sultanas and currants;*
> *half lb skinned almonds to chop;*
> *quarter lb of suet;*
> *1 lb plain white flour;*
> *2 big Bramley apples;*
> *mixed spices (ground ginger, mixed candied peel,*
> *   ground nutmeg, cinnamon)*
> *bottle of stout;*
> *six eggs;*
> *one orange;*
> *one lemon;*
> *soft brown sugar.*

The battered preserving-pan came out, the old recipe was followed, and we all stirred the mixture, and then cooked it on the Rayburn for seven or eight hours. Mum still made the mincemeat herself. After we left she wrote, *'The puddings look very good in the larder. I have to put clean greaseproof paper and foil on each one – which reminds me, did I pay for the greaseproof and foil?'*

In the days before Christmas we took over the shopping, rushing up and down Ridgeway with plastic carrier bags full of all the things that, for so long, she had struggled to carry. We gave ourselves over, as much as we could, to making life the same as it had been since Dad died. In Job's words, *'If only I could go back to the old days.'* Mum used to sing, to the same effect, the spiritual from the cotton fields of the Deep South: *'Gone are the days when my heart was young and gay ...'*

In her diary she wrote some fateful words of Edward FitzGerald, perhaps by her mistakes in some of the words even adding power to these lines in the *Rubaiyat of Omar Khayyam*:

> *'The moving finger writes*
> *And having writ moves on;*
> *And neither piety nor wit*
> *Can cancel out a line.'*

Mum had a stream of visitors over the New Year. *'Monday was lovely. Dorothy Score came at two thirty and didn't leave until five. We had a beautiful fire. On Tuesday Joan Hurn and Nan Matthews came to cups of tea, and the coal-man visited. They answered the door to him and made the tea. It was very funny. They shut the back garden gate after the coal-man left.'*

In February 1995 Florrie, Dad's last remaining sister, died.

At Easter we stayed with Mum. We managed to take her to eight o'clock Holy Communion. The strain was telling on her. On the following day she wrote, *'John and Judy gone. Sad.'*

The pace quickened. I visited her every four or five weeks. Judy and I both stayed with her at Whitsun. Mum would write something in her diary after these visits:

'Lovely time. John gone. Sad';
'John here. Good. Lovely three days';
'I cooked dinner. We sat in garden. Very hot';
'Lovely time with John and Judy.'

At the end of July and in early August, Judy and I took a holiday in the North. The heat was stifling over all the country. One evening when we telephoned Mum, she was very confused, fluently producing non-existent but uncannily plausible words and phrases. On a Sunday evening, in the middle of August, we arrived at Number 10 to spend a week with her. In her diary Mum recorded what we did that week, as her spirits rose day by day:

Sunday: John, Judy and Bracken arrived from Scotland.
Monday: J, J and B – swim and roast beef.
Tuesday: J and J took me to hospital: good test. Swim, drive to Plymouth.

Wednesday: J, J and B at Ayrmer cove, the Magic Beach.
Thursday: J and J took me to Mount Gould Hospital, foot clinic.
Friday: J and J visited Jane for the day.
Saturday: J, J and B at Ayrmer – swim. Hot. Chicken.
Sunday: 8am at St Mary's. J, J and B gone. Very sad.'

Mum looked well when we left.

As the years had passed, Mum felt the benefit of our visits for a shorter and shorter period after we left. The last entries that she made in her diary were on Sunday the tenth of September.

On the morning of Monday the eleventh Mum was sitting at the breakfast table in the kitchen, writing her weekly letters.

'The greatest sadness is when you can't write letters any more,' she said to me a year later, in hospital. *'I always tried to write something, even when nothing interesting happened in the week. As Dad said,* "Habit is ten times nature." '

Midway through a sentence in her letter to Judy and me Mum slumped forward onto the table.

As had happened eighteen months earlier, Mum's friend Nan had decided to call on her on Monday morning that week because she was not able to make her regular visit on the Tuesday. Every Tuesday afternoon for years the two of them had banked up the fire in the sitting room and eaten frangipanis for tea.

But this Monday Nan looked through the glass in the inner front door down the passage to the kitchen and again she realised that something had gone wrong. She contacted Roger Triscott, the local builder who had taken such good care of Number10 for so many years. He got into the house through the sitting-room window, and for the second time Mum's life was saved by her good friends. They called an ambulance to take her, unconscious, to hospital.

Through these two good friends Providence was watching over Mum and our whole family.

PART THREE

13

A Last Gift

ON AN IRON-FRAMED BED, in a side room off Ward 12, Mum lies on a Pegasus air mattress. The electric motor of an air-compressor hums very quietly and, every so often, it gently inflates or deflates one or another of the lungs of the mattress. The 'Friends of Ward 12' have raised the money for the hospital to buy more of these mattresses. Ward 12 is a special place. It has many grateful friends. The flow of air changes the contours of the bed and reduces the risk of causing bedsores. Mum was already suffering from one when she was moved to the specialist unit here from a ward in a general hospital.

Outside, about sixty feet from the window of her little room, stands an immense horse chestnut tree, covered in fresh green leaves. The first white and saffron flowers are opening. Mum watched the tree's leaves turn brown and fall, along with the conkers, last autumn. She saw the tree's branches, bare against the blue winter sky. You can look at a tree for a long time.

Mum has lain on this bed for six months. She is turned every two hours or so from one side to the other by members of a group of skilled and dedicated nurses and assistants. She is paralysed on her left side, the effect of the stroke that she suffered in September. She cannot feed or clean herself.

Mum's speech is a little slow, soft but clear. Sometimes her mind is muddled, but often it is completely lucid. Sometimes she sleeps deeply, sometimes fitfully. After a deep sleep this morning, her mind is alert.

'I've been over nearly all of it now,' she tells me. *'I'm happy.'*

I never know what to expect. As I walk along the corridor towards her room I try to be silent and invisible. Today I manage it. All the nurses are far away at the other end of the ward. As I creep up to the door of Mum's room, I hear music. It comes from an old black and white television set. The nurses switch it on when Mum is in the mood, and today it is playing quietly.

Mum loves old films. She is chuckling to herself contentedly and peacefully. I stand outside the door for a while and listen. Mum suddenly gives her infectious laugh, a completely happy and healthy sound, and from the television there is the pained cry, *'Mr Grimsdale...'*

It is Norman Wisdom's voice. He is starring in one of his films, made in the 1950s or early 1960s, which have given us so much joy at home over the years.

Mum and I watch the last few minutes of the film together before we begin to talk.

Three Christmases pass. The end of Mum's life is drawing near.

One day in her final spring when I arrive, all the nurses and assistants are on their rounds. There is no other visitor in Mum's bay, and she and the other five elderly ladies there are asleep. After arranging some flowers and watering her plants, I take a chair and settle down beside her bed. There is a gentle murmur of activity and conversation around us, floating in from the other parts of the ward.

After ten minutes or so, Mum opens her eyes. Even this takes an effort now. Slowly she manages to focus on my face, and then on the flowers, and then again on me.

'Good afternoon, Mother,' I say. This ritual has sustained us for thirty months. For a moment, there is a flicker of a smile, but today no words.

Mum's head rests on the white pillows, and her eyes half close. I sit there beside her, and the quiet, concentrated activity continues in the ward.

Then Mum's eyes open wide and she looks directly at me. Without being able to make a sound, she suddenly mouths some unexpected words to me:

'Two more for the Russians.'

And those are Mum's last words to me. I cannot restrain my laughter and it echoes down the ward. It is a joke that goes back forty-five years to early 1953, to the terrible days when Stalin still ruled in Russia and controlled Eastern Europe; when millions of Russians and others worked as slaves in Communist concentration camps. In a way, they were the lucky ones. Forty million people or more had already died because of him. He threatened us with a similar fate.

On an afternoon in February that year, a few months before the Queen's Coronation, when I was seven and my brother five, we stood after school at Mum's side in Mrs Willcocks's sweet-shop in Ridgeway. As he served us with lemon sherbets, her dour, withdrawn son looked down at us and uttered the sinister comment, *'Two more for the Russians'*. It was a month before Stalin's death.* And those words, so macabre in themselves and in their original intent, we turned into a joke that never failed us over the years. It is Mum's last gift to me in this life.

Sister Val and one or two of the other nurses and Marie, the tea lady with her trolley, bustle up to our corner. They are

---

* See *Two More for the Russians,* forthcoming.

puzzled and look at me uncertainly. Then they see Mum's eyes shining with joy and triumph as she watches me laugh. It is impossible to explain the meaning of this laughter to Sister Val and the others. For a moment they smile at us, and then drift back to their work.

Mum's head settles back on the pillows and her eyes close. She sleeps for the rest of my visit.

Ward 12,
Mount Gould Hospital

I hang between life and death,
And life calls
And death calls,

And which I should choose
I know not,
I will not.

I rest in the hands of God,
And man must
Wait and pray.

14

'What can't be cured...'

THERE IS MORE to facing death than old jokes and laughter. Much of it you wish had never happened. Sometimes you wish that your own life had ended before all this was happening before your eyes. Perhaps, occasionally, you wish you had never lived at all. Yet, as Mum's mother used to say, *'What does not kill you makes you stronger.'* Perhaps you will be grateful for what you have received when it is all over. After all, everything ends.

Mum and I had for years often spoken about death, and what preceded it, and what followed it, as we believed. Mum loved life but she was ready for the end, even before she went into hospital and suffered a stroke there.

During her thirty-two months in Ward 12, between her stroke and her death, Mum turned over in her mind what had made her, and us, happy. She told me stories that were new to me, as well as reviving many memories that we had shared so often. She brought out songs that we had never heard before. She recited verse, and went over the plots of novels: *Our Mutual Friend* (Dad's favourite Dickens novel, she told me), *Nicholas Nickleby,* and *Pride and Prejudice.* Above all, she reviewed her life and the lives of her family and friends. She was preparing herself for the end.

In the years in hospital the question of wanting to die did not arise for her. It is only when death is absent that you want or do not want to die, or both, sometimes simultaneously. But during her last three years, death was present, with her and with us, all the time.

It was like living in a dream, sometimes a nightmare. But there was none of that horror of being in the wrong place, or struggling to get somewhere else, which gives some nightmares their edge. We were in the right place.

All of this is beyond the reach of reason and justice and the law and 'rights', of rationalists and judges, of Parliamentarians and academics; it cannot be entrusted to those who have any interest in *power*.

The only thing to do is to wait and be silent and attend to everything that happens. It is the greatest mystery in the world. You, too, will go this way.

Mum was taken ill three weeks before I left one job and became self-employed. That change was to prove my liberation. Mum helped me to cross my own Styx from one way of life to another.

Suddenly I was more or less the master of my diary and time. I could spend a lot of time on visits to Mum. I went there on seventy-three trips between October 1995 and May 1998. Twenty-two of the visits were day trips, and fifty-one lasted for three or more days. Judy came when she could. My brother and sister-in-law faithfully visited Mum. At Christmas and Easter and on holidays all four of us gathered at Mum's bedside.

The routine hypnotised me. Out of bed by six o'clock, for a day-trip; breakfast; train and tube across London; a pot of coffee, with toast and marmalade, in the comfortable, friendly, rather shabby lounge of the Great Western Hotel at Paddington station, now lost to modernisation, and become soulless; watching out for familiar landmarks from the train – the canal,

the Vale of the White Horse, Athelney and King Alfred the
Great's refuge; picking up a bunch of flowers at Plymouth
station; a taxi ride to Mount Gould Hospital; walking up the
stairs to Ward 12; the bustle in the ward as nurses and order-
lies tidy up after the early hospital lunch; and, at last, the walk
along the corridor, greeting the nurses whom I now know so
well, some at the central desk and others as I go to the end of
the ward.

I turn the corner into the bay where Mum's bed is placed,
opposite Ivy's.

'Good afternoon, Mother.'

*'Good afternoon, John. I've been expecting you. I prayed that
you'd come and now you are here. It often happens. When you came
in I got the same old thrill.'*

I pull up a chair and arrange my belongings. I go along to
the cupboard in the entrance hall and take out a vase, fill it
with water at the hand-basin near Mum's bed, and do my best
with the flowers.

When I am staying at Number 10 I can bring flowers from
Mum and Dad's garden, their flowers: violets, camellias,
celandines, viburnum, New Dawn roses, bluebells, apple
blossom, lilac, and kaffir lilies. But any flowers are welcome to
Mum in hospital, especially those that are sweet-smelling; and
above all, freesias. Often I ask the flower shop at Plymouth
station to have the flowers ready for me when I arrive: every
minute counts. Its owner belongs to the Salvation Army, and
he makes me a special bouquet for Mum. He understands what
ill people need. He has visited the ward with other Salvation-
ists for a service of hymns and prayers at Christmas or Easter.

Carefully, I bring the freesias over for Mum to smell.

'Lovely.'

Mum asks after Judy, who is working at school today. She
always asks after Judy straightaway.

*'Judy's lovely. Give her my love. She's a godsend in an earthquake.
She's wonderful. She knows what to do in a predicament. Judy holds
our family together …*

'I remember collecting chestnuts with her in Greenwich Park... And blackberries. I wouldn't want to be a blackberry if Judy were around... I've always loved Judy.'

Mum goes over so many incidents and conversations that she has had with Judy over the years.

She remembers her own mother.

'She told me that, because I came along last in the family, when she was forty-three years old, she couldn't feed me herself. Forty-three is old *when you have already had seven children. She said that the only thing she could do for me was to give me limewater to drink, so that I would have good teeth and strong bones, and it came true...*

'Poor old Mother, I was such a baby. I cried when she said, "I've forgotten to give my little girl her cabbage." I was daft, and terribly spoilt... It'll be lovely to see her again. I want to see her again now, even if it's just for five minutes... She was always working, always there, with her love and lovely ways. She loved doing anything for us all. She got up at half past four to get the fire going and get breakfast ready for the boys going off to work at the china clay pits. It was a long walk for them to Lee Moor.

'She loved Christmas. On Christmas Eve, as she was making mince-pies, and lots of visitors were coming and going, she used to drink a glass of stout, and she would put a red-hot poker in it to warm it up if it was a freezing day.

'She always looked so smart on Christmas Day in the new clothes we had given her. I used to enjoy going to Pophams, with its thick carpet and its glass counters with their wooden drawers, and buying her a lovely blouse.

'She kept all her treasures and presents in a pink satin box. It had four legs, and had been a chocolate-box. She had a few little pieces of jewellery. There was a diamond-and-sapphire brooch, and another of tiny rubies and mother-of-pearl. She kept her father's Bible there. She used to hide peaches in that box when my father brought her some from Major Strode, from the orangery at Newnham House. She loved peaches unashamedly, *the only thing she kept to enjoy herself and did not give to us.*

'We had so many happy times...

'I do hope that Mother enjoyed her life. I hope that so much. She and Father were together for all those years, and scarcely had a cross word.

'At the end of her life, in the War, she was lying ill in bed, in the Blitz, and then she opened her eyes and said, "Do stop looking at me so much, Grace!"

'She wasn't eating very much by then, but we gave her a little good, expensive food. Mrs Penny and Bill James from next door gave her a bowl of brown eggs from their hens.

'Dr Brown attended her during her last illness. She told me not to cry for her when she'd gone. "Regain your equilibrium" was how she put it.

'And she just slipped away. I went downstairs from the bedroom, leaving her asleep, and then, when I went up again, she'd gone.'

'We got her ready for the coffin. I dressed her in a clean nightdress, and we put roses in the coffin, from a Madame Butterfly rosebush planted under the dining-room window. They were beautiful blossoms. I put in her special prayer-book, with the big print, and lay it with a rose on her breast in the coffin. I made the mistake of inviting Agnes, Harry's daughter, to come in and see Mother – she was Mother's first grandchild; she was looking so lovely and peaceful, but Agnes felt her cold skin and she broke her heart, crying. Agnes loved her so much, and didn't understand why she was cold now. I didn't warn her about that.

'Mother left me £8 and her rosewood writing table…

'While I was in India with Dad and you, Jack and George stained the table with their shaving tackle, but it came up all right when I polished it. They threw away the pink satin box, although I'd put all of Dad's letters in it for safe-keeping, tied in bundles with ribbon… Jack and George were very rough-and-ready, down-to-earth men…

'I'd give anything to see Mother, just for five minutes…'

And gently, half under her breath, Mum sings the song, 'Love is the Sweetest Thing…'

She drifts into silence for a while.

Mum begins to think of her father.

'Father used to get angry with me. We had an old wind-up gramophone, and every piece of romantic music and sentimental song used to make me cry. Father said that I was watery-eyed ...

'Father had a hard time in the dockyard in Devonport in the First World War. "A carriage horse, doing the work of a carthorse," *Dr Stamp said. But later he went back to work as butler at Newnham House ...*

'After his heart attack, Mother kept him on a diet of white meat – chicken and fish. She was furious when Hilda gave him eggs and bacon once. Mother helped him live sixteen more years' ...

Mum suddenly looks me straight in the eye.

'I'm not ruining your life, am I?'

'You're a lovely part of our life.'

Mum smiles broadly.

'Don't smarm me, will you? Life is difficult, especially when you've got an old woman of eighty-seven for your mother.'

We laugh a lot.

After a pause, Mum talks about her father again.

'At Christmas I gave Father a big beaker of peppermint mintoes, tied with a ribbon. He loved mintoes. He'd been plump and jolly-looking when I was a little girl, but now he was thin.

'He always wore a bowler hat when he went out and he used to raise it to ladies. "Without manners", he used to say, "we are nothing." He was steadfast, stern, and caring; a good man ...

'Mrs Damerell owned the house where we lived in Moorland View, and Mother and Father rented from her. Her husband was a farmer. I used to go each week with our spaniel Sam, to pay the rent. Ten of us lived there at Number 12, and Mrs Damerell told Mother how neat and tidy she kept the house for so many of us ...

'The Salvation Army band used to come and play under the lamp-post in the street, collecting pennies. They are wonderful people. I remember them helping soldiers in the First World War. Bless their hearts ...

'Further along the road lived Mr Fowle. He had a dog, called Jack. When he came out into the back lane to call Jack in for his dinner,

the children used to shout after him, "Mr Fowle lays eggs"... We were awful. He was such a nice gentleman. Then there was an Italian couple called Barnesconi. He was an officer in the Royal Navy and he had a beard, and used to shake his fist at us when we were too noisy...

'All the children used to play in the back lane. It was stony, and muddy in winter. We used to make a little fire, and cook the peel from a Christmas orange in a tin to make marmalade. There was a linhay there and we used to climb in its rafters.

'We used to play in the road at the front of the houses around the lamp post, in the dark, with a torch, "Jack, Jack, show your light!" and "I sent a letter to my love and on the way I lost it". Lots of girls and silly laughing...

'Edie Paul was my friend at the baby school. She sat next to me. One day Miss Blight said to her, "Edith Paul, put on your thinking cap," and Edie replied, "I can't, Miss; I've only got my 'shanter'."

'Mrs Webber lived next door to us and she was very mean. She sent me on an errand, and only gave me a rotten apple for doing it for her, and she dug out the rotten bit with her thumb. You don't expect that from your neighbours... They were lovely russet apples, too.

'Once she hid behind a curtain in the hall when the rent-collector came. Her little boy told him that she had gone to Plymouth. The man said, "All right, sonny, but tell your mother to take her feet with her next time she goes."

'Ethel Tucker lived at Number 1. She lived there all her life. We were in the same class at school. I still miss her. I'd love to see her walk round that corner now saying, "I will lift up mine eyes unto the hills, from whence cometh my help." She used to say that to me when Dad died...

'We all sat around the dining-table at Number 12, five boys and three girls, expecting poor old Mother to serve up something nice, and we always had a good meal...

'Edie Law used to come and knock on the front door and ask Mother, "Can I come into your miggle room, Mrs Janood, and play with Nacey Noo?"'

Mum often talks of her brothers and sisters.

'*Harry was fourteen years older than me. He was in the War, but he managed to buy me some gloves that winter at the end of 1914 when I started school.*

'*Edie was next, twelve years older than me. She used to take me out in the pram for Mother. She bought me a mauve blanket-coat and a bobble hat for school. Everyone loved that coat ... I really loved school when I got used to it ...*

'*Later I was Edie's bridesmaid, with a pink dress and a pink hat. I was only eleven and a half. She was a lovely sister, but I hardly knew her.*

'*Jack was next, almost eleven years older than me. He was a* gentle *man, but he had a sad life after Iris Williams broke off their engagement. She was my best friend then, and Jack said to me,* "Keep your mouth shut. You are always causing trouble by talking too much." *He went to the Julian Arms in Underwood and got blind drunk when she threw him over. He was never really happy sharing the house all those years with George after Mother died and I got married ...*

'*Hilda was nine years older than me and two years older than George. She used to help George with his fruit and vegetable stall in the market in Plymouth. George got shabby and lame and he had terrible ulcers on his legs. Once some young girls laughed at him at the bus stop in Plymouth, and Hilda told them off.* "Do you realise that you're laughing at my brother? You're **not** to laugh at him. My brother's a gentleman."

'*When George died, I found a photo of Mother in his wallet. He kept it with him all the time. I hadn't realised how much he loved her. Poor old George, he used to keep all his sadnesses hidden under concrete blocks and try to be cheerful. George was the odd one out among us all, really. I was always worrying about him.*

'*In the market Hilda was so popular that people used to queue up at George's stall to talk to her. She and Edie used to flirt terribly with Army sergeants in the First War. When they were out with their sergeants, George made fun of them by calling after them,* "Come home quickly. Mother wants to borrow your boots!"

They were furious. They used to frighten me when I was a little tacker by opening the wardrobe in our bedroom and bringing out a plaster of Paris cast of a human hand, all shining white in the darkness...

'*Three years after she married Fred, Hilda had a terribly long labour giving birth, and, after John was born, she said she'd never have another baby... We all loved John, and he blamed me for spoiling him. At his birthday party he recited,*

> "It's my birfday today, and I'm eight,
> which makes me grown up and sedate;
> so I'm having my tea all alone,
> excepting for Teddy and Joan."

He was a lovely little boy, a mass of golden curls.

'*When he got married, I used to embarrass him terribly by telling Margaret all about that. Poor John used to turn bright pink. I often think of him now...*

'*Arthur came next after Hilda, only five and a half years older than me. He was the best of us all, and he died when he was only thirty-four years old.*'

Mum cries. Thinking of Arthur always does this.

'*It's because of Arthur that I'm so keen on people being nice to each other. You never know what's going to happen, or what you're doing to people...*

'*Wally was two years younger than Arthur, three older than me. He looked up to Arthur. And Arthur encouraged Wally a lot, because he was a nervous boy. They were lovely friends to each other. They went out looking for birds' nests together...*

'*Then I came along and messed everything up for them all.*'

Not so, I tell her.

'*You mustn't gild me over. I'm fed up with* me, *a bad tempered old sinner...*

'*Then, when I was twelve, Mrs Damerell sold Number 12 Moorland View and we moved to the new council houses at Stone Barton, on the other side of Plympton. At Number 12 we still had oil lamps, and one was made from an artillery shell from the War. Mother used to trim the wicks every afternoon. But we had electricity at Stone Barton from the start.'*

The nurses come to make Mum more comfortable, and to turn her onto her right side. We know them so well now.

It is as if we have always known them. It is as if this life that we share with them will never end; but it will.

I walk along the ward and have a word with one or two of the patients and some of the nurses. In the day-room, where the more active patients can sit and read or watch television, I gaze out of the window and look at the estuary of the River Plym.

At low tide there is a wide expanse of sand, smooth and sparkling, laid down over the years by the waste of quartz and feldspar carried there by a moorland brook from the china clay works at Lee Moor. It stretches from the Plymouth side of the river to the woods that lead up from the rocky shoreline to Saltram House. This afternoon there is a high tide and the blue, slightly choppy waters glisten in the early afternoon sun. Once or twice, in her first year here, I was able to take Mum outside in a wheel chair, so that she could feel the breeze on her cheeks and see the wonderful view.

No one is in the day-room today. There are pictures on the walls and a bookcase, with a vase of paper flowers standing on it. It has the atmosphere of a sitting-room, frozen at some date in the 1970s, when the patients here and most of the visitors would have been in their late middle-age, still able to run their own home and enjoying life, with grown-up children and, perhaps, young grandchildren. Everything about the room seems to fit in here, and it is a comfort.

Winged chariot

With horses, it's their teeth;
With dogs, the hazy spreading
Cataracts or loss of spring
That give the game away.

With us, it's hi-fi sets,
Their matt metallic finish fading
With the years,

And on them photographs,
And dust, of children and grandchildren,
Christmases and weddings.
All that hope

Greets us when we visit
Seldom. Do the vinyl records spin,
The speakers sound?

Or do they form an altar
To the past
On which their life,
And all that gave it sense

Is offered up?
With videos and DVDs
Our turn's next.

15

'...on my way, rejoicing'

THE CURTAINS AROUND Mum's bed rustle and are drawn back. I see that Asha has been helping Mum. Asha is a Nepalese nurse. She and Mum sometimes talk about India and Mum's years there with Dad. They get on well together. Asha told Mum that her name means 'hope'.

'The other night Asha didn't come to me when I needed her. All the hope *I'd placed in her was lost.'*

Asha and Mum laugh together at the joke. Mum watches her walk away down the Ward.

'Asha's a lovely person,' Mum says. *'She gets worried about me sometimes. She's* honourable *and a very sharp, sturdy little person. I wish I were* honourable. *She loves her mother. She's bringing her to England for Christmas.*

'I told her about Dad's bungalow at Saugor, and the green leaves of the range creeper that covered all its walls. The Indian robin used to build nests in it; it had a red tail instead of a red breast. Asha was very interested...

'I loved it when Dad laughed. I loved to hear his Cornish jokes and to hear him laugh... He loved the joke about the man selling newspapers who used to call out "News of the World – and all the other places"... *I'd love to see him and hear him have a good laugh now.*

'He used to say, "O what a troubled web we weave

When first we practise to deceive."

133

'*Everything that Dad planned worked out well. If only I had let Dad guide everything, it would all have been better. I went in where angels feared to tread. How much he loved you boys. He was so proud of you both ...*

'*Dad was generous and gentle, always on the side of the loser. He was the best thing that ever happened to me ...*

'*On one of our first walks when we were courting, we had lunch at the Skylark Inn at Clearbrook. Dad had a bread roll and cheese. I can see him eating it now ... I was overjoyed that, later on, he let me buy him a pint of beer. I had lemonade ... Dad proposed to me at Lee Moor Gate, on the edge of Dartmoor ...*

'*In India, he loved to have* "rumble tumble" *for breakfast, sitting with me on the verandah. That's what he called scrambled egg. He used to break the brittle toast into pieces by putting the flat of his hand on it, on the plate ... Dad looked so lovely there in his officer's uniform ... I asked Kundan, our bearer, why they served us toast without the crust. I always liked the crust. Kundan said,* "We eat the crust, memsahib." *I felt so ashamed and small, and worried about what I'd said ...*

'*Our garden was full of flowers. The mali used to water them every day ... Beautiful Indian schoolgirls used to walk past the bungalow in their school uniforms and we would hear them singing ...*

'*I always worry about putting my foot in it.*

' "Worry is your middle name," *Mr Hefford used to say to me. He owned the shoe shop in Ridgeway.* "You've got the most worried look I've ever seen," *he said. He tried to make me laugh. When I was a little tacker, he used to say to me,* "I like to see you in the morning, Grace, and then I have said 'grace' before meals." *Then, when I grew up he said,* "You haven't got your mother's dainty feet, Grace," *but Dad said that I needed a big foundation of size eight shoes because I was five feet ten inches tall. Dad always comforted me, the dear of him ...*

'*Wasn't it lovely when we lived at Venton Cottage? I used to put you both in the pram, and push you up the lane by the wood. We'd all meet Dad off the bus at Sparkwell coming back from Plymouth with the weekly shopping, and then we'd walk together down that wonderful lane to the cottage and the fire, and kippers for tea ...*

'We had a lovely garden at the bungalow at St Ives. Dad loved working in it and cleaning out the chicken-run. There was a big border of lupins and dahlias.

'On Guy Fawkes Night Dad ran around the garden with sparklers to entertain you...

'He went up to Plympton to look for a house and he found Number 10 Moorland Road. It was convenient in every way for us, and for you both to go to Plymouth College...

'Dad was always keen for you boys to go there. He was very clever, and got his Higher National Certificates in the Army. You made us both burst with pride with all you did at Oxford...

'Do you remember the little barrel of cider that Dad used to have standing by the door in the kitchen each Christmas... and the bottle of Dry Fly sherry that you used to buy him for his birthday? And how he used to buy you both raspberry and banana milkshakes at Mr Crooks' shop when we were at the caravan at Challaborough?

'Don't forget all the lovely outings with Dad, the walks, and train rides, and Paignton Zoo, and the theatre, and picking whortleberries at Princetown on Dartmoor... Take good care of Dad's M.B.E.

'Later on [when Mum says this, she means the time when Dad was suffering from Huntington's chorea], he and I loved picking up chestnuts at Windwhistle Wood with Rusty. Dad loved doing that.

'I thanked Dad for a lot of things a couple of days ago when I was going through them all, for more than ever before... I'm so glad that I have him for my husband...

'He was lovely, wasn't he?

'I'm looking forward to seeing Dad again. He was a lovely husband and father... He was the best thing that ever happened to me. I was almost too happy with him, but I didn't have long enough with Dad, only twenty-eight years...'

And Mum's face takes on a special tender look. And for a while all is quiet around us in the ward, with the nurses walking to and fro, and their footsteps muffled by the springy grey linoleum, and the sun shining across the floor and the beds, and no one speaks.

'I'm sorry,' I say at last. We sit in silence.

I'm feeding Mum some English strawberries cut in quarters, with caster sugar and clotted cream.

'Are you enjoying them?'

'I was going to say, "Can a duck swim?" I should jolly well think I am! Dad used to say that giving me one chocolate was like feeding a donkey a strawberry'...

We play a game.

'I spy with my little eye, something beginning with "P",' Mum says.

I try pillow, peas, pillowcase, pills...

'No. Pneumatic ptarmigan,' says Mum triumphantly. She tries again with 'P'.

I rack my brains. 'Post, pyjamas, pane of glass...'

'No. Pharmaceutical pterodactyl,' she tells me with her eyes twinkling.

Mum loves words.

'My father told me that I had the gift of the gab,' she says.

Words divert her and entertain her. She used to love crosswords, especially the *Daily Telegraph* prize crossword on Saturday.* We try a spelling game. She sets herself *diaphanous* and gets it right.

'It makes me feel exuberant,*'* she tells me, and spells it.

Time and again in these thirty-two months Mum would bring out the right word, sometimes immediately, sometimes after deep thought. *'That lady who visited the ward yesterday was* bonny,*'* she said once, exactly catching her rosy, plump cheeks and healthy complexion.

By choosing the right word, Mum showed that she was still in the world, a force to be reckoned with, and that she could still make her own distinctive and original contribution to life. She relished this gift, savouring spellings and pronunciations,

---

* By a twist of fate I won the prize in this competition on what would have been Mum's one hundredth birthday.

the shape and feel of words, colourful and amusing idioms and turns of phrase.

'*That barley water was worth a guinea,*' she told me. And, '*The thought of that pudding doesn't set me on fire.*'

She loved to bring out rather old-fashioned slang words:
'*What a* shemozzle',
'*Fancy having a* dial *like that*',
'*Do you remember Tony Hancock's* cake-hole *and* hooter',
'*It's not easy to get all this into my old* top-knot',
'*Here I am,* grousing *again*',
'*I've had a good* doss'.

Sometimes Mum said to me, '*I'm going in the head,*' but on others occasions, '*I'm not losing my grip.*' She certainly showed that the latter was true although, during all those months, she had the use of only her right hand and arm, and was, as she put it, '*a bag of bones*'.

She used interesting and varied words: *stealthy, terse, fervent, merry, prim, raucous, bombard, flippant, injurious, predicament, cumulus, agile, irksome*... She told me that she had had a 'riotous' birthday. Speaking of the Queen's constancy and reliability in the worst of circumstances, and of her refusal to bend to the ways of Babylon, Mum said in admiration, '*She's a prude. We need more prudes.*'

The afternoon is beginning to slip away. Jim, a retired merchant seaman who visits his wife every afternoon, and has done so since her stroke three years ago, is enjoying the horse-racing on the television. Marie, the tea lady, wheels her trolley along the ward, stopping at each bed and pouring cups of tea for patients and their visitors. She is due to retire quite soon, and is not looking forward to it.

I help Mum with her tea.

'*Excuse my* slurping,' she says. '*Not many sons would have to do this for their eighty-seven year old mother. I'm an albatross around your neck.*'

16

'A Ring of Faithfulness'

MUM STILL GETS lots of visitors.

There is no one of her generation still alive in the family, but her nephews and nieces, and Dad's, come to see her when they can. Friends from Plympton visit.

But two people, both in their mid-sixties, have emerged as Mum's most frequent visitors.

From Mum's side of the family there is her niece Mavis, Edie's daughter. She was widowed many years ago and is now sixty-five years old, not in wonderful health but still walking on Dartmoor, swimming in the sea off Plymouth Hoe, and reading and writing poetry. She is always full of fun and often has the patients and staff in uproar with her jokes.

And from Dad's side of the family there is his nephew, Jack, Florrie's second son. He was born in the same cottage as Dad in Jack Lane in Newlyn and was named after him. As a little boy, Jack wrote regularly to Dad in India. Jack is very fond of music, singing in his choir, poetry and the German language. In his fine copper-plate hand he used to write out poems from his favourite authors for Mum.

Both Jack and Mavis love the corny jokes that are so dear to Mum and so powerful in raising her spirits. One or other of them is often with Mum when I visit her. They work out between them when they will visit, a roster to ensure that

Mum has a visitor as often as possible. I have seen the way that they take care of her. They treat her like a mother.

On one occasion, when the nurses were delivering Mum her supper and she looked disgusted with it, Mavis said, 'It's lovely,' and pretended to begin to eat it.

'That's Mavis's style of getting me to eat,' Mum told me. *'Give me a reason why I should say it's lovely because Mavis says it is,'* but she began to drink the soup and to reminisce.

Often Mum and Mavis sing together and they enjoy themselves a lot. *'Silly songs,'* Mum says, *'A load of rubbish, like* "Bye, Bye Blackbird".' They sing deliberately flat, and laugh.

'We're very much alike, Mavis and I,' Mum says. *'Both daft. When I saw Mavis and Debbie, the nurse, whispering together, I called them* "the wicked women's club", *and, boy, did they laugh! They had been worrying about me, but, when I made that joke, they knew that I was all right.'*

'Jack told me that he'll never leave me, he'll keep coming right till the end,' Mum told me one day. *'In the old days he used to take me from Number 10 to Plymbridge to see the kingfisher, and he told me the other day that, from now on, he'll remember me every time that he crosses the bridge. He'll touch the bridge and pray for me. He's such a dear. He said,* "You're never going to get rid of me. I'll keep visiting you wherever you are." *He could see that I needed comfort.'*

Then, as the end came near, Mum said, *'Jack came, and immediately everything was all right ...'*

At the end, when Mum could no longer speak, she gave Mavis a deliberate, slow wink, as if bidding her farewell and thanking her for all the laughter they had shared.

'I don't know what I'd do without Jack and Mavis. They are a ring of faithfulness ...

'The world would be a sad place without the Mavises and Jacks ... And it's not over when I'm gone. The family is still there, and everyone has still got to be connected with each other ...

'I love Mavis and Jack, and they know it ... I told them.'

Roger Beck, the curate from St Mary's, glides quietly around the corner into Mum's bay. Her face lights up and she welcomes him, *'I didn't know that it was Wednesday.'*

During Mum's three years in hospital, Roger used to come to Ward 12 to celebrate Holy Communion with her. He would bring a special service sheet, with the main parts of the service printed boldly in big type on one page of paper. Mum could hold it in her right hand.

Another patient in the ward, Olive, and her husband, Harry, used to join in the services sometimes. By an extraordinary chance, Olive suffered from Huntington's chorea, as well as the effects of a stroke. Mum may never have realised this coincidence.

On one occasion she said to me, *'Thank Mr Richards for being such a good vicar at St Mary's, for loving the village so much.'*

Sometimes some of the nurses (Sister Val and Barbara), or two of the patients, Dick Triscott, and his wife Pixie, and Olive, and her husband Harry, join in the service at Mum's bedside, but today it is just Roger and Mum, with me.

Roger gives her a copy of St Mary's parish magazine.

'Thank you. I'll read it later,' Mum says politely and clearly.

They talk quietly as Roger lays Mum's side-table with a white cloth, and arranges on it the little Holy Communion chalice and patten and a prayer-book, just as he had done when he had visited her at Number 10, on the second Wednesday of the month.

Mum asks him to use one of her favourite prayers at our service today:

> *'O God, who hast prepared for them that love Thee*
> *Such good things as pass man's understanding,*
> *Send into our hearts such love toward Thee*
> *That we, loving Thee above all things,*
> *May obtain Thy promises which exceed all we can*
> *desire,*
> *Through Jesus Christ, Our Lord. Amen.'*

She attends intently as Roger leads the service and joins in the prayers and says 'Amen' strongly and firmly. Afterwards, while Mum has a talk with Roger, I go for a walk down the ward.

When Roger has left, Mum says to me, '*Lovely things happen through being a Christian. Being in church makes you happy. It would be nice to have Jack here for the service. He prays with me, too.*'

When the time came, it was Roger who gave Mum the last Christian rites, Holy Communion and anointing with holy oil. He saw her safely on her final journey to the life of the world to come.

What Mum endured in those thirty months sorely tested her. Some things, like being given a bath, were almost more than she could bear. Her bones ached, and her fragile skin grazed against the bath, pinching her. It made her cry. Sometimes her faith supported her, sometimes she felt troubled.

'*I didn't think that life would end like this, did you?*' she said. '*I thought it would phase out easily.*'

Once she said to me, '*Where is Jesus? How can He help me? Where is He?*'

Another time, she told me, '*I haven't felt the Lord for a while.*'

And, again, '*Why should God treat me thus? I'm in a black tunnel, and I've got to come out of it. It's driving me mad. I don't feel I've done anyone any wrong. Why should I have to go through this?*'

There is no answer.

The occasional despair passed, and Mum again felt God's presence in a comforting way. She prayed for '*peace at the last*'.

She told me, '*I've been through some awful things, but it hasn't all been awful. It all depends on Jesus. He's the only way to get through everything.*'

Mum never gave up praying for us all. '*I want you both to be really healthy and well. I pray for that all the time. It's like an ache, an ache in my throat.*'

Remembering the kingfisher at Plymbridge, she said, '*Never mind. We've got to leave this world sometime. Thanks be to God for the glory of it.*'

She saw all good things as signs of God's presence. '*I've been thinking of apple blossom,*' she told me once, just as I arrived; and, again, '*I've been thinking about the ponies on Dartmoor.*'

'*People come around the door and restore my faith,*' she told me. '*If I ever did anything right in my life, it was by accident. "Remem*-ber not our sins, O Lord." *The terrible thing about life is what you ought to have done and did not do ... Jesus is our Rock and Salvation ... There is only God. You've just got to put your trust in Him. I try to ... Prayers help us to get through life.*'

One day in the early months I took Mum to the day-room in a wheel-chair. I gave her lunch as we looked across the estuary. At the end of our talk Mum closed her eyes for a while. Opening them, she said, '*Help me, Dear Lord, to go on my way rejoicing.*' Again, she told me, '*I prayed, "O, Lord, forgive me for not continuing to be positive."*' We often prayed the Lord's Prayer together at the end of visits.

On another occasion Mum told me, '*I dreamt that I was at my own funeral. I said to everyone, "Don't be sad. I'm on my way to my Lord Jesus."*' Quoting hymns, she said,

'*Jesus, lover of my soul ...*

'*I heard the voice of Jesus say, "Come unto me and rest" ...*

'*Jesus, the very thought of Thee with sweetness fills the breast ...*

'*Don't cry for me. I'm ready to go on my way to my Lord Jesus. Nothing is impossible where Jesus is concerned ... It'll be all right as long as Jesus gets us right in the end ... He's got a big job to do.*'

Jesus had been absolutely the centre of Dad's faith. During his years in India, Dad had underlined in pencil the name of Jesus in the first line of many of the hymns in his hymnbook, making a note of when each was sung at St Peter's church, Saugor. The talk about Jesus takes Mum's mind back to Dad.

'*I wonder what Dad's doing now ... He might be looking at the Rayburn in Number 10, or walking along Jack Lane in Newlyn. We can't tell ...*

'Where did Dad actually die? I remember. It was at Moorhaven Hospital... When Mr Matthews was vicar at St Mary's, I asked him for advice about Dad. Dad had to go to the hospital, and he seemed to have settled. Mr Matthews said, "If he's happy, don't have him shifted around." So Dad stayed there, and he was not desperately unhappy, he was not.'

Mum adds the last three words with great force. Her eyebrows, still black although the hair on her head is now completely grey, rise emphatically and her brown eyes open wide, showing how convinced she is that Dad's last three years were as good as they could be.

'Remember your visits to him. You went to see him three times a week for three years and every day for his last three months,' I say. The memory comforts her.

'Thank you, John...

'I remember going there on the double-decker bus... Pat Fallack used to sit with me in the front seat, upstairs. We wanted to see all the flowers in the lanes on the way there. We started work together at Yeo's when we were fourteen. Pat was a lovely friend. She was working as a helper at Moorhaven when Dad was there. It did me good to see her shining face, with her brown eyes and dimples. She was a kind person, and she had her sadnesses too.'

Mum recalls Auntie Kath, Dad's youngest sister, who died at Moorhaven ten years before him.

'Poor Kath... She liked coming to us on Sundays for her bath and tea from her lodgings in Plympton St Maurice...

'In those days, with meat rationing, we used to have Lemco gravy with roast potatoes and cabbage, and Yorkshire pudding. Kath said it was even better than a joint. Then for tea, I used to make a little 'speciality' in a sponge-tin. She liked it after her bath. That was our Sunday together, and church.

'Later, I used to make a custard tart for Dad to take when he visited Kath at Moorhaven. Poor Kath, she was a lovely, gentle person. She had such a sad, short life...'

Time is racing on.

'*I hate it when you start collecting your belongings together to go,*' Mum says.

'*I'm not quite ready to die yet. I'll have to part with you all, but one day we'll all be together again.*

'*I hope that you'll bring Judy with you next time, and that you'll be able to go to the Magic Beach, and have a dip... I think about those days on holiday at the caravan all the time.*'

Mum nods towards the snap of Dad, standing on the beach, empty after everyone else has gone home, looking out to sea.

'*I call that picture "Contemplation",*' she says.

And then she looks at a postcard, propped on her bedside table, from Mr and Mrs Vicary, and their children, Robert and Carol. We used to meet them every summer for ten years at the caravan.

'*I wish they were nearer,*' she says. '*Very faithful people. I love their faithfulness, like comrades in a war.*

> "Comrades when danger was near;
> Faithful whatever betide;
> Whenever dangers appear
> My comrade is there, by my side..."

'*Faithful friends, and a happy family...Dear God, forgive me, and help me to be worthy of it...*'

And this is what Mum and Dad taught me.

St Paul, reflecting on what he learnt through God's revelation to him in Jesus Christ, wrote that of the three great virtues – faith, hope and love – the third is the greatest; but without courage and loyalty they are nothing.

That is what they taught me.

My time is spent. I pack my belongings in my canvas London Library bag.

'*You're a very tidy person,*' Mum says. '*I can see you now, folding up your pyjamas... Thank you for all the loving care you've shown me...*

'*This is a lovely ward. They are all such dears...*'

And, with a final wave, I slip away and rush down the stairs to the taxi booked to take me to the station, and so back to London. On the train I sleep.

And none of us, and none of the doctors, can tell how long this will continue.

The months slip by, thirty-two months in all.

Skin-deep

Three skins, three days.
One skin each day
Removed; and not
By Genghis Khan.
But she who bore
Me now torments
Me as she lies
And waits.

The stroke half killed
Her, but left quick
Those feelings which
Are torn from me
And flayed.

Each day I sit.
We talk and cry
And laugh and pray.
Three days; enough.
It's done, as much
As I can do.
'To save yourself,
Away'.

17

'Such sweet sorrow'

FOR TWO AND A HALF YEARS and more I had found a unique escape (a release from all the tension that we went through) in my Russian language lessons, in what one of my teachers called *'the Russian music of words'*. On Monday or Wednesday I would go up to London to attend my classes with a succession of brilliant teachers. They always refreshed me.

On the first Wednesday in May 1998, after half a day's work, I felt jaded and off colour. I went home and wandered around the house listlessly. Something stopped me from going up to London for my conversation class. Normally, I would have felt sure that seeing Sasha our teacher and all the members of the class would lift my spirits, but that afternoon I decided against going.

Soon after five o'clock, Sister Val telephoned to say that Mum might not last long. Judy took me in the car the few hundred yards to our local station, and I just managed to catch the last express train from Paddington to Plymouth, the 7.35. I treated myself to dinner in the restaurant car. On the margin of a page of the newspaper I was reading, I wrote Dad's words to Mum in January 1945, when he left her in London after their honeymoon to return to India, *'Parting is such sweet sorrow.'* I tore off the scrap of paper and put it in my jacket pocket. I found it months later.

At Newton Abbot the train was delayed for a while when a drunk accosted the guard. The police were called. I did not reach Ward 12 until 11.30pm.

My brother and sister-in-law were already at Mum's bedside. They sat on one side of her bed, and I on the other. Mum's breathing was loud at first. Taking turns, we spoke quietly, close to her 'good' ear.

Nurses Ann and Liz turned Mum, and her breathing eased, growing slighter and slighter. Who can tell what she took in, but we continued to talk quietly to her in turns. Everything became still and peaceful, in her, in us, in the ward.

At the end, I hardly realised what had happened; yet suddenly everything was different. We sat beside Mum for a little while longer. We had a talk with Nurse Ann. A doctor came to certify the death. We kissed Mum goodbye. By 2.30 am we were back at Number 10 and went to bed. I blessed God for His goodness to me in Mum and Dad, and repeated, as I went to sleep,

'Parting is such sweet sorrow.'

Judy arrived from London. She and I visited Ward 12 to collect the doctor's statement of the cause of death and Mum's belongings, and to bid the nurses farewell with flowers.

One of the nurses took us over to the little chapel where Mum's body was resting. For a long time Judy stood at the foot of the bed, as if in conversation with Mum. I kept out of Judy's line of sight, at the back of the room. Later, Judy told me, 'She was there; waiting for me... There was a lot to say.'

The funeral took place six days later.

The flowers were purple and white, as Mum had wished. Many of the nurses and helpers in Ward 12 were present.

On the coffin, at the last moment, I also laid a small bunch of lily of the valley from the back garden of Number 10. They had flowered and spread there steadily over the forty-eight years since Dad had bought the house. Mum and Dad both loved them. On a card I wrote, *'To our much loved and much loving Father.'*

It brought the two of them back together at the end, and for ever.

Epilogue

'... the means of grace
and the hope of glory ...'

We're born in Adam,
Take his flesh,
We wither and we die,

But we are given
Each a chance
Of endless life in Christ,

(Who, dying once, was
Raised for all)
To find our peace in Him,

A life that's endless,
Saves our soul,
Reverses Adam's fall,

To rest forever
In God's care,
Where death has power no more.